Logotherapy

New Help for
Problem Drinkers

Logotherapy

New Help for Problem Drinkers

James C. Crumbaugh, Ph.D.
William M. Wood, M.D.
W. Chadwick Wood, M.D.

Nelson-Hall nh Chicago

Library of Congress Cataloging in Publication Data

Crumbaugh, James C
   Logotherapy.

   Bibliography: p.
   Includes index.
   1. Alcoholism—Treatment. 2. Logotherapy.
I. Wood, William Martin, 1924-   joint author.
II. Wood, William Chadwick, joint author.
III. Title.
RC565.C78   616.8'61'06   79-18635
ISBN 0-88229-421-0

Manufactured in the United States of America.

10   9   8   7   6   5   4   3   2   1

For Teresa, wife who gives
meaning to life (JCC)
and
Natalie, devoted
wife (WMW) and
mother (WCW)

Contents

Foreword

I have made it a principle in my life to leave everything to an expert in the field and, therefore, to raise my voice only in case I am convinced that I am an expert. From this, the reader may understand how reluctant I was in the first place when invited by the authors to say a few words about their book by way of a foreword: In no way can I regard myself as an expert in the field of alcoholism.

What should I say, what could I say? Should I say that I don't drink any alcoholic beverages? I don't see therein a merit; I just can't stand the taste of alcohol, and this dislike is not even the result of upbringing or being conditioned (frankly speaking, I don't know whereof it is the result). And from the viewpoint of logotherapy I don't know much more about the origin and treatment of alcoholism than what I have read in Dr. Crumbaugh's writings plus in a dissertation and a report. As to the dissertation, I am referring to Dr. Annemarie von Forstmeyer's study at California Western University, and as to the report, I am referring to a series of case histories that Dr. Eva Kozdera once compiled, upon my request, as the basis for a paper I had been invited to read at an international congress on alcoholism. Dr. von Forstmeyer could show that about 90 percent of severe cases of chronic alcoholism were caught in an existential vacuum to a marked and significant degree as measured by Dr. Crumbaugh's "Purpose in Life" test. And Dr. Kozdera could show that her patients were able to overcome their alcoholism only if there was a cause, or another person, for whose sake this would be done; and, contrariwise, if either suddenly disappeared (say by loss of a beloved or by loss of a worthwhile job), a relapse into alcoholism was observable.

I wouldn't like to be misunderstood: I am not saying that the frustration of one's will to meaning is "the " cause of alcoholism. As are most phenomena in psychiatry, or for that matter in medicine at large, alcoholism is of multifactoral genesis. Focusing on one single pathogenic agent, or—as I would like improvisingly to call it: "mono-etiology"—should be left to the quacks (if, for no other reason, to allow and enable them to capitalize on their one-sidedness by creating therapeutic fads and fashions that easily enter the consciousness of the broad public, even if only for short periods of time).

What I want to convey to the reader by this cautious and skeptical remark is my conviction that even though I do not consider alcoholism as being caused (at least not exclusively) by the existential vacuum, filling up this vacuum may well be of primordial therapeutic value—nay, a prerequisite for therapeutic success, and in any event a decisive component in the rehabilitation of the chronic alcoholic.

And I could not imagine any author to be more competent than Dr. Crumbaugh in this area. I first met him in 1961 when I was Visiting Professor at Harvard University's Summer School, upon Gordon W. Allport's invitation, and I, in turn, invited Dr. Crumbaugh to join my seminar on logotherapy and to report on his research in empirically validating logotherapeutic concepts and in making them quantitatively measurable. Later on, I saw him again on several occasions, among others when I was invited to lecture at New Orleans' Loyola University (afterwards he gave me an unforgettable guided tour through the French Quarter).

Anyway, I have come to know him as a person unique in blending a triad of properties that reminds me very much of a formulation I came across when reading the German classic of sociology, Georg Simmel: Somewhere he comes up with the sequence, "Life—more life—more than life." Similarly, Dr. Crumbaugh impresses me as someone who is a therapist—and a therapist, at that, with a sound and solid scientific foundation on which to base his therapy—and a therapist, last but not least, who deliberately allows his personal warmth to pervade his scientific work. In short, Dr. Crumbaugh, as I see him, is a synthesizer of himself, *i.e.,* of the three aspects of his own personality that form a trinity: therapist—scientist—humanist.

Viktor E. Frankl, M.D.,Ph.D.

Preface

We all have our own ways of "copping out"—running from life when it becomes too frustrating. Alcohol abuse is merely one way. Regardless of the theoretical causes of problem drinking, those who have fallen into its trap can get out only through a deep and abiding determination to do so. This determination will exist only if one has found a powerful motive based on a real meaning and purpose that give life significance and make recovery worthwhile.

The aims of this book are, first, to demonstrate to the problem drinker, his family, friends, loved ones, employer—to you, wherever you fit in these categories—the nature and causes of alcohol abuse; second, to present the types and sources of help for it; and finally, to offer a new and powerful source of assistance that can enable the problem drinker to find real meaning and purpose in his life and thereby a sense of personal identity, pride, and self-fulfillment.

This new kind of help will furnish the motive to become a part of that successful group of whom it is commonly said, When the going gets tough, the tough get going. It will enable the problem drinker to face frustration, overcome obstacles, and meet life's problems without crawling inside a bottle. It will help him to help himself, and it will show him how, once recovered, he can have an important part in helping others to achieve the same goal. Wherever you fit in the picture in relation to the problem drinker—whether you are he or someone who cares about him—this approach will offer you an important role in recovery, and in the recovery of others, if you want it.

We would not kid you. This new technique, in which the first author specializes, is no panacea. It does not "cure" anyone (the real cure comes only from within the motivated individual), and it does not help everyone. Nothing does. But it can help most people with bright minds, who are free from organic brain damage and severe mental illness, and who have a sincere desire for help.

It is called *logotherapy* (from the Greek *logos*, "meaning")—treatment through finding new meaning and purpose in life. Originated by the famed Viennese psychiatrist, Dr. Viktor E. Frankl of the University of Vienna Medical School, it holds that man's chief need is to find a real life meaning, and it offers techniques of achieving this.

The present work first presents a picture of the medical, physiological, and psychiatric side of alcoholism and then offers a special application of the principles of logotherapy to the problems of problem drinkers. If you or anyone of yours fits this category, it is written for you.

Part I, authored by Doctors Wood and Wood, offers a technical (though popularly written) presentation of the biological side of alcoholism and problem drinking. It may be skipped by readers not interested in these aspects of drinking problems, but we believe that understanding them will help one to deal more effectively with the psychological side, described in Part II by Dr. Crumbaugh.

This is a self-help book. While it can be more easily applied with the aid of a therapist or counselor, you can do this alone if you are motivated to have a better life and if you follow carefully the instructions given herein. If you do have a guide, the work will go faster, and you may be saved from the temptation to quit in a period of weakened motivation. Either way, what you do for yourself in applying these principles will be the keystone of success.

While the book is directed primarily toward problem drinkers, the same principles apply to people with many other types of problems of everyday living. The principles will work in a wide variety of situations for anyone who follows them rigorously.

In this connection these principles are especially applicable to *problem eaters*, for the psychological factors in the etiology of overeaters and overweight conditions are almost identical to those in problem drinkers.

We would like to emphasize that *if you have any symptoms of mental or emotional illness*—such as abnormal or unusual fears, excess anxiety, depression, thinking which many others consider illogi-cal or delusional, unusual withdrawal from the social contacts of everyday life, an unusual degree of difficulty in adjusting to the frustrations of life, an unusual degree of difficulty in concentrating or in sleeping—*or any physical symptoms*, like dizziness, headaches, gastrointestinal upsets, backaches, pain in any organ, and so forth, or if your friends seem to think you have any of these symptoms, you should first go to your physician for a thorough checkup. You should then follow any recommendations or referrals that he makes before trying to help yourself by this or any other book or self-help method, although you may be able with his approval to do both at the same time.

Symptoms mean that you need professional help of some kind, and your doctor is the best judge of what kind. You should not attempt to go it alone. And in fact, each of us is often the poorest judge of our own mental and emotional state; for this reason, your physician would never attempt to treat himself. So if you or other people have thought you have any symptoms, go to your doctor. If your problem is problem drinking—as will be the case for the majority of readers, since this book is directed toward them—you are likely to have some of the psychological symptoms we have noted, as they represent conflicts from which you are copping out by alcoholic escape. And if you have been at this very long, you are likely to have some physical symptoms, so the chances are very good that you need your doctor first.

A final word to all therapists and counselors in the fields of mental health, emotional problems, and personality difficulties: Regardless of your therapeutic orientation, you will find the approach of logotherapy adjunctively helpful in the cases of many patients or clients. This book can aid you in applying this approach.

Acknowledgments

Portions of this book have been taken, essentially verbatim, from the first writer's earlier book, *Everything to Gain: A Guide to Self-Fulfillment through Logoanalysis,* with permission of the author and of the publisher, Nelson-Hall Company of Chicago. This material appears in the present book in parts of Chapters 4, 7, 8, and 12.

The writers wish to express deep appreciation to Prof. Dr. Viktor E. Frankl, the founder of logotherapy, for reading the manuscript and for valuable suggestions which have been incorporated into it; and for his graciously writing the Foreword.

We are also very indebted to Elaine Edmunds, R.N., widely known specialist in alcoholism therapy, for the quotation on the cover jacket.

Part I

The Psychiatric, Medical, and Physiological Aspects of Alcoholism and Problem Drinking

Chapter 1

Alcoholism:
Cause and Effect

William M. Wood, M.D.

My colleague and close personal friend, James C. Crumbaugh, Ph. D., has honored me by requesting that I contribute to this book. The subject of alcoholism, its causes, and methods of intervention have interested me since 1942. I will attempt to express my views based on thirty-two years of medical practice, the successes I have observed, the failures I have witnessed while wondering to the extent of amazement at the struggles of my fellow human beings.

My interest in the matter of alcoholism began when I was a medical student and was fostered by a request of my father. At that time, he was attempting, as an interested, concerned family member, to help his brother to redirect his life, discontinue his drinking, and perhaps recoup some of his multiple losses. Every medical student has had a visit from his family when he attempted to point out and demonstrate how the family's emotional and physical contributions had helped produce a medical genius. Fortunately, I was not able to make such a profound statement to my father, but I did seek out some of my professors, one of whom was chairman of the Department of Psychiatry. He was wise, honest, and helpful, and after an hour's session, he suggested that I spend my elective in the Psychiatry Department and participate in a research project being conducted with alcoholics. I accepted his advice and reached several conclusions at the completion of the elective. I made several promises to myself and to my family. One was that I would not pursue any specialty that required my involvement in the treatment of alcoholics.

My professional activities consist of twenty years of family practice; a residency in psychiatry, followed by a position as staff psychiatrist with the Veterans Administration; and at the present time, Chief of the Psychiatry Service. The tenure with the VA has encompassed a period of twelve years and approximately four years professional association as Clinical Director of the State Hospital and director of community mental health centers. Throughout all these professional activities, I have recognized my inability to keep my promise to avoid the alcoholic. Much has been learned by me and other members of the medical profession during the last thirty years; however, many questions remain unanswered.

I remember vividly the establishment of the Yale Center of Alcohol Studies and the quarterly *Journal of Studies on Alcohol.* I have watched the progression of events and have gleaned thoughts from a great many publications, including those of Dr. E. M. Jellinek, a leader in the movement and one of the founders of the Yale Center. Jellinek was the first to publish the "disease concept" of alcoholism, and he also developed "a natural history of alcoholism," which originated the concept of loss of control and separated the alcohol addict from the nonaddicted drinker. I have witnessed the acceptance of alcoholics in our community hospitals, which resulted when society gained new insights into the etiology and promulgation of the disorder and took responsibility for its own contribution thereto. I have also witnessed, and at times participated in, rather heated discussions regarding the etiology and the most beneficial therapeutic methods.

The disease concept has enabled study to continue and helped to develop explanations. But none of the explanations has convinced me that there is an inborn organic defect responsible for the disorder. In fact, it appears that the attempt to explain and define alcoholism as a *disease* as well as *illness* has contributed to the confusion. In my opinion, the medical profession does not even have a clear definition of this term. One turns to the current medical dictionaries for a definition, or *the* definition, of *disease,* and finds that it is "a definite morbid process having a characteristic train of symptoms; it may affect the whole body or any of its parts, and its etiology, pathology, and prognosis may be known or unknown." *(Dorland's Illustrated Medical*

Dictionary, 25th ed. 1974). One can readily see that this definition is all-encompassing and not definitive. Physicians conceive of disease as having an etiology, a defined progression of symptoms, and a treatment. However, the etiology of many conditions—for example, cancer—remains undefined, even though the progression and treatment are defined.

Physicians believe the disease concept provides a framework within which members of the medical profession can take responsible action. To consider alcoholism as disease does provide an organizing principle; however, much discussion and many recent developments indicate that the process in alcoholism is psychological and not physical. This position applies not only to alcohol, but to drug addiction as well. The World Health Organization's committee on drug dependency regards all drug dependency to be primarily, if not entirely, a psychological disorder.

Resolving the question of whether alcoholism is or is not a disease, in my opinion, is neither pertinent nor necessary in a successful therapeutic intervention. The matter of "who is and who is not healthy" is one of an ill-defined and personal evaluation. Those of us involved in the delivery of mental health services witness behaviors that are quite bizarre, sick, ineffective, and poorly directed, yet the individual participating in this behavior may appear quite content, obviously receiving the emotional gratification desired. To establish standards for others' behavior is not in the realm of reasonable or sensible professional activities.

Many theories have been offered as explanations for alcoholism—for example, a physical explanation, a psychological explanation, a psychoanalytical explanation, a nutritional theory, a genetrophic theory, an endocrine theory, a brain-damage theory, a metabolism theory, an allergy theory and, last but not least, a theory of sin, which alleges that an individual's abhorrent activities and self-destruction are directed by mystical and unexplained powers. This list is only partial, but it seems apparent that the multiplicity of theories is related to the absence of a well-defined and overall agreement as to the cause of the problem.

It is my opinion that certain individuals seek out the age-old tranquilizer, the most readily available and socially acceptable one: alcohol.

I consider this activity to be an attempt to relieve pain or distress of an intrapsychic nature. Apparently, man throughout the ages has sought methods to produce a feeling of well-being, an altered state of consciousness; obviously, he is driven by the "pleasure principle." His activities to establish and maintain relief and "happiness" often are short-lived and lead to self-defeating results. Sigmund Freud was of the opinion that alcoholism was a result of strong oral influences in childhood; he also described the mood alteration and consequent redirection of thought processes characteristic of alcoholism and emphasized that alcohol enabled an individual to get away from reality. Karl A. Menninger said a self-destructive drive is the prime component of the disorder; Knight formulated the psychodynamics of alcoholism as related to a personality characterized by excessive demands for indulgence; Adler described the alcoholic's characteristic feelings of inferiority and insecurity and his need to escape responsibility; McClelland wrote of frustrated ambitions, suggesting that the alcoholic may have an enhanced need for power but is inadequate to achieve his goals. In reviewing these theories and in recounting therapeutic involvement with patients, I recall successes in which no identifiable treatment was responsible for the success.

It is my opinion that the alcoholic must be approached as an individual who does not wish to be an alcoholic or enjoy the resulting pain and discomfort. He is a victim of both unresolved intrapsychic problems and external factors and contributing forces. In attempting to understand these unhappy, miserable, compulsive people, we must look at their lives in a longitudinal fashion, recognizing their deprivations, their successes, their failures, and all aspects of their day-to-day living. As one assumes this task and facilitates the individual's self-assessment, one learns of many episodes in which the patient sabotaged his own successes for unexplained reasons. In addition, factors not under the individual's control influenced his or her drinking, and frequently the patient identified at an unconscious level with a person of similar problems and characteristics.

It is my conviction, formulated during thirty-two years of experience, that much of the time spent in an attempt to understand alcoholics and help them return to a more productive life is wasted. The only successes I have seen were persons who were able to develop their own concept of God, their own determination of what things they desired and considered of value, and their own direction. It is distressing to see an individual flounder and fail in attempting to establish goals and to continue this self-defeating activity—which is, in fact, failing at failing. It must certainly be distressing for the person himself to be unsuccessful with failures. If a person chooses to fail, one must assume that the choice is related to ambivalence or inadequate ego structure.

It has been my observation, based on clinical experience, that an individual in the throes of alcohol abuse can, with understanding and assistance, accept the reality that "his problems are in *his* head," that the answers to those problems are also "in *his* head," and that the activities of the helping person are a matter of sorting and assembling. Once the individual can accept these premises, he can determine what *is* of value and what *he* wishes to obtain, and then success is on the way. I am of the opinion that once an individual has made this redirection, with conscious awareness of his behavior, alcohol no longer is a problem for him; he might well be able to use it in moderation without destructive effects.

I see alcoholism, not as an entity or illness in itself, but as a disorder demonstrated by compulsivity and undue preoccupation with alcohol. As one considers this statement, it becomes obvious that the "preaching" abstainer is struggling with a preoccupation, a fear of loss of control, and that he demonstrates some of the characteristics of the so-called alcoholic. Actually, the behavior of both alcoholic and "preacher" is the result of many factors, some of which are unconscious and not understood by the individual; these unconscious forces may represent poorly directed strivings and frequently are opposite to the thought processes.

The role of unconscious forces is important and frequently overlooked by do-gooders. Alcohol does not produce thoughts; yet both drinkers and do-gooders often attempt to explain verbalizations, behavior, and failures as the result of thoughts produced by the chemical. Alcohol is in no way guilty of this; it serves only as a deinhibitor that allows thoughts to emerge and expressions to surface.

My efforts to understand this malady, to participate in a helping role, will continue, and at this time logotherapy appears to offer the greatest hope and promise for this work.

Chapter 2

The Medical and Physiological Side of Alcoholism and Problem Drinking

W. Chadwick Wood, M.D.

The Medical Side of Alcoholism

No problem in modern medicine challenges the ability of patients and physicians more than that of alcohol abuse. Alcohol not only has wide-ranging effects on the various parts of the body, but it also inhibits the patient's ability to care for himself, further accentuating the physical problems. Impairment of judgment may result in accidents involving the alcohol abuser himself, or innocent bystanders or family members. Alcohol abuse is a frequent cause of automobile accidents and, surprisingly, is suspected to play a role in a number of aircraft accidents as well. Alcohol is involved in thousands of cases of murder and more thousands of cases of suicide each year. It is conservatively estimated that some nine million persons in the United States today have a serious alcohol abuse problem. The time lost from work, family disruption, personal inconvenience, hardship, and illness resulting from alcoholism and its effects on others are perhaps beyond easy reckoning. Attempts directed toward helping these individuals cope with their physical illnesses and assisting them to cease use of alcohol will pay rich dividends for all concerned.

Alcohol and Its Effects on the Body

The ingredient in alcoholic beverages that produces their effects on the body is known by the chemical name ethanol, or ethyl alcohol. It may be produced by fermentation of grapes or other natural substances

9

or made chemically by a process known as distillation. Fermented beverages are less than 15 percent alcohol, and distilled beverages are about 50 percent alcohol. Alcohol brings about changes in mental function and inability to use the muscles of the body in a coordinated fashion by acting on the brain, what physicians refer to as the central nervous system. The timing and intensity of these effects depend on many factors, among which are the amount of alcoholic beverage imbibed, the concentration of alcohol in the beverage, whether food was in the stomach prior to drinking, the body weight of the individual, the time period during which the drinking occurs, and the person's individual reaction to alcohol itself.

The route by which alcohol leaves the body is through chemical alteration of ethyl alcohol in the liver by certain chemical substances called enzymes. One of these chemical substances, known as alcohol dehydrogenase, is critical in this process. Since the amount of this material in the liver is limited, the rate at which alcohol leaves the body is fairly constant, being about 10 milligrams of alcohol in each 100 milliliters of blood during each hour. In other words, a normal individual would metabolize, or chemically eliminate from the body, one and one-fourth quarts of beer in five or six hours.[1] It is particularly important to realize that sleep or exercise does not speed up or slow down this elimination of alcohol from the body and that they exert no "magic effect" in speeding up recovery from imbibing alcoholic beverages.

Alcohol is basically a depressant of the nervous system, and what individuals experience as a "stimulating" effect of alcohol is actually a result of this depressant effect. Careful scientific studies have shown that decreased ability to do precise tasks with the muscles of the body is evident after the first alcohol ingestion. As more and more alcohol is drunk, the individual goes through a series of physical changes, ranging from mental changes—including a release of tension and increased willingness to mingle with other persons—to a decreased ability to use the muscles of the body in coordination and a decreased ability to use good judgment. The individual becomes less inhibited and more uncoordinated, and his reaction time lengthens. Later the individual becomes confused, dizzy, unable to walk without imbalance, and unable to speak without slurring of words. As higher and more medically dangerous levels of alcohol in the body are reached, the individual may become less conscious, even more uncoordinated, and eventually comatose. Extremely rapid ingestion of large amounts of alcoholic beverage may result in coma, which may in some cases be fatal. Vomiting and a fall in blood pressure at high levels of alcohol consumption constitute serious dangers to the intoxicated. A decreased ability to operate machinery of all types exists at all levels, becoming more pronounced as higher levels of blood alcohol are reached.[2] The effects of alcohol may be made worse by the use of tranquilizing or sedative drugs at the same time, and alcohol, in turn, may enhance the effects of the other drugs. Serious mental and physical deficiencies in performance and behavior may be the result.

Alcohol irritates the lining of the stomach and may produce bleeding from the stomach lining itself or from a preexisting ulcer in the stomach or the duodenum. Alcohol has adverse effects on the liver: it may cause the body to deposit fat in that organ and may well eventually result in a loss of liver substance itself and its replacement by scar tissue, a process known as cirrhosis. Individuals who consume large amounts of alcohol may well neglect to eat a proper diet and may become vitamin deficient, resulting in many diseases of malnutrition. Inflammation of the pancreas, a gland located in the abdomen near the stomach, may result in abdominal pain, formation of cysts within the abdomen, or abscesses in this gland. Alcohol-related changes in the blood can result in anemia and decreased ability of the blood to clot. Over a period of time, alcohol can damage the heart muscle and decrease the heart's ability to perform properly. Both the nerves of the arms and legs and the muscles of the body may be affected detrimentally by alcohol. Damage to the brain itself may result from abuse of alcohol.

A condition known as delirium tremens, or "DTs," may result when an individual ceases to drink heavily. Individuals who experience this dramatic condition become tremulous, confused, disoriented, and sleepless. They move about in an agitated way and remain confused and ill for a variable period of time, following which most recover after an interval of sleep. This condition is often a serious medical problem requiring careful attention to intravenous fluids, control of diet, sedation, and careful observation to prevent complications such as pneumonia. About 10 percent of patients with delirium tremens have convulsive seizures, referred to in the past as "rum fits." Hallucinations may occur in delirium tremens, and it is of prime importance to prevent the patient from injuring himself or others during this most critical period.

Steps in the Drinking Pattern Leading to Alcoholism

Identifying the individual who will be an alcoholic is a challenging and difficult task. There have been attempts to categorize the progression of individuals through various steps that eventually lead to the alcoholic stage made familiar in movies and television programs. Many individuals begin using alcohol at irregular intervals, perhaps at parties or other social occasions; later they take alcoholic beverages at increasingly frequent and regular intervals. As time passes, more and more alcohol is deemed necessary by the individual to produce the desired mental effect. This is because people develop a tolerance to alcohol—that is, an amount of alcohol that originally produced a given effect on the brain and body has less effect as an individual drinks more and more heavily. As the disorder progresses, episodes of loss of consciousness may occur; these "blackout spells" are very significant as danger signs for severe alcohol abuse. Eventually the individual is unable to voluntarily cease alcohol intake, and periods of drinking alone may ensue.

Throughout this sequence of events, the individual experiences more and more difficulty in adapting socially to his family and work commitments, further accentuating the endless circle of more pressures, more alcohol abuse, and more problems dealing with his responsibilities. During this stage, the individual may give untrue explanations for actions related to drinking and is likely to turn in a poor job performance. He probably will become progressively more isolated emotionally, thus worsening his ability to find help for his alcohol abuse problem. Perhaps it is best to think of alcoholism in terms of a condition that progressively decreases the ability of the person involved to cope with himself, his job, and his interrelationships with others. Any of the previously mentioned physical problems may be the end result of uncontrolled drinking. Personal injury due to accidents or suicide attempts may further harm the individual, whose ability to adapt to changing and stressful situations has already been badly compromised by alcohol.

Thus, abuse of alcohol results in damage to the body itself and to the brain, which is charged with judgment and reason. Individuals lose the ability to perceive their problem and exhibit poorer judgment in all areas of their everyday life and work. This loss, combined with the isolation of the individual from those very persons most concerned with him, generates a situation that is likely to worsen with time. Rational approaches to the treatment of alcohol abuse must concern themselves with all these areas and attempt to comprehensively aid the individual, both emotionally and medically.

The Psychiatric Side of Alcoholism

At the present time, alcoholism is best considered as a disorder with a spectrum of manifestations. The individual who is an alcoholic may have episodic periods of drinking, which may result in intoxication once a week, once a month, or less frequently. He may drink daily and may show tolerance to the effects of alcohol, requiring more and more drinking to produce the mental effects he desires. Alcoholism has both physical aspects, as previously described, and psychiatric aspects. For effective treatment, neither group of problems can be neglected. The modern "team approach" to psychiatric problems involves the psychiatrist, internal medicine physician, social worker, psychiatric nurse, occupational therapist, family, and other interested workers in the total care of the patient in order to touch all areas contributing to his abuse of alcohol.

Probably each individual who drinks to excess has a different background of personal experience that has led directly or indirectly to his drinking problem. Similarities among groups of alcoholics have been noted, but each case must be approached individually. Certainly society condones much of the alcohol abuse that leads to more serious drinking problems. The cocktail party, office celebration, and collegiate gathering are frequently scenes of heavy drinking. Alcohol abuse is often encouraged by those who know nothing of its ill effects and who understand little of the personality makeup of the individual being encouraged to drink. Many persons find a release of tension when using alcohol but fail to realize the difficulties alcohol abuse creates in adjustment to job and family. Many who develop drinking problems have a family member or friend who used alcohol in dealing with social problems. Some psychiatrists believe certain individuals use alcohol to punish themselves, to vent their hostility inwards. In many cases, the precise cause of alcoholism is not known. In others it can be speculated upon but not proven. The many theories of alcohol abuse indict the drive to injure oneself, insecurity, blocked life plans, a search to reduce tension and conflict, an attempt to reduce anxiety states, a learned response to dealing with various problems, and other possible causes. A chemical basis for alcohol addiction is not proven at this time.

Treatment of Alcoholism

In past years, efforts to treat alcoholism as a multifaceted disease problem have taken various approaches. The use of drugs such as disulfiram (Antabuse) to inhibit alcohol ingestion is complicated by the unwillingness of some patients to take the Antabuse itself. Adjunctive use of sedative or tranquilizing agents such as chlordiazepoxide (Librium) does not solve the basic problem of why the individual has abused alcohol. Group therapy has been helpful, and Alcoholics Anonymous in particular has been beneficial to many alcoholics. This combination of group therapy, compassionate interest, and readily available assistance to deal with problems draws on the strength of its many counselors who have had personal experience with alcohol abuse in the past. Perhaps an important key is the ability of the alcoholic individual to relate to others on a person-to-person level and to find individuals with similar problems who are willing to help him. He can thus verbalize his conflicts and compare experiences together with others who have a similar problem.

Provision of definite goals for therapy is important, and a day-to-day approach rather than vague long-term goals is frequently necessary. In particular, the therapists and family must react realistically without hostility to relapses and continue with patience and persistence to assist the individual in breaking what has for him become a consuming pattern of dependence—mental and often physical—on alcohol. The individual must learn again to deal with life's problems realistically and not turn to alcohol as escape or self-punishment. With this type of treatment program, many persons can be helped, many can be cured, and all can find other individuals to help them in this readjustment task.

Part II

The Psychological Side of Alcoholism and Problem Drinking

James C. Crumbaugh, Ph.D.

Chapter 3

Motivation:
The Key
to Recovery
from Alcoholism

Motivation is the real key to recovery from problem drinking. If you have such a problem, your natural reactions to this statement might be, What has motivation got to do with alcoholic problems? Why should I as a person with a drinking problem be interested in motivation? Of course I am motivated to achieve the good things of life, but I can't get them because of this drinking problem. Motivation is wanting something, isn't it? How is wanting things I don't have going to help me overcome drinking and get them?

The key to it all is that you have wanted to receive without giving. You have wanted the results without having the life values and meanings that produce them. You have wanted a certain effect without understanding how to manipulate the cause that will produce this effect. You have wanted to keep going toward certain goals, but you haven't had the *kind* of life motive that makes it worthwhile and meaningful to withstand whatever pressures and to overcome whatever obstacles you have to in order to achieve the goals without copping out through the use of alcohol. Let me prove it all to you.

First let's examine the psychology of human motives. There are two basic kinds of needs, biological and psychological. The biological needs are those such as hunger, thirst, sex (which is really complex and on the *human* level more psychological than biological), respiration, and elimination.

Now when we are hungry, little else matters. Any frustrated biological need will become dominant over all other needs at the time, as the late great psychologist Abraham Maslow has shown. In societies where millions of people are deprived of biological necessities—for example, India, where tens of thousands are born on the street, live on the street, and die without ever having had the protection of a roof—the biological needs are the primary concern of life.

But in American society, even in deprived areas, it is rare that one cannot with reasonable effort obtain the biological necessities of food, clothing, and shelter. We may not have steak to eat or furs to wear, but we can have nourishing soup and warm apparel. In America, even in the lower socioeconomic groups, most of us can fulfill the biological needs.

Now when the biological needs are fulfilled, we then turn to the psychological needs, and they in turn become paramount. They are the needs for love and affection, social approval, status, recognition, response from others, mastery, new experience—in short, the needs that involve establishing a personal identity, becoming Somebody, fulfilling self-esteem. Notice that all of these needs involve other people. You could fulfill all of the biological needs, even sex, alone; but you could not fulfill any of the psychological needs, without involving other beings. Some individuals can fulfill them in relation to lower animals (pets), but they personify the animals as if they were human.

Yes, everybody has to have somebody in order to find a personal identity as Somebody. And this is what really makes life worthwhile and gives us the strength to go on when the going gets tough. Being Somebody does not mean that we must be rich, famous, or great. Most of us won't make that. You may, but I certainly won't. It does, however, mean having importance. Because we all are important. But we have to be important *to* someone. That's what makes us Somebody.

When we are Somebody we can stand frustration if we have to, the frustrations of everyday life that come to everyone. Everyday living is full of frustrations for us all; there is *no* way we can avoid them. We can only go on in spite of them. Sometimes we can remove them by direct effort; sometimes we can get around them; sometimes we must bear up in spite of them. In all cases, coping with frustrations takes work on our part. If we have enough going for us to make the effort worthwhile, we will stand our ground; if not, we will cop out.

If we feel that we are Somebody, that we have something in life going for us that makes our life worth living, we will do our very best to withstand the pressures and go on to achieve that which gives our life this meaning. But if we feel the opposite, that we have no real purpose in it all, why shouldn't we give up? Why shouldn't we cop out with alcohol or whatever means of escape we find handy?

Alcohol is just one method of escape that people use. Many cop out with other drugs, or by sleeping all the time, or by reading or watching TV all the time, or by working all the time. We'll find some way to run if we haven't got a strong motive to achieve something that makes us Somebody and that gives us a reason to go on in spite of life's frustrations.

There is nothing really new about the psychology of all of this. It has been recognized from earliest times. The ancient Romans said that everybody has to have an *apologia pro vita sua* ("apology for his life")—a reason for living. The French have said that everyone needs a *raison d'être* ("reason for being")—a reason to justify his existence, which means that he must feel like Somebody. Psychologist Abraham Maslow said everyone needs some form of *self-actualization*—some outlet for his desire to fulfill his potential as a unique individual. Young people have expressed the same need by the phrases "I want to do my own thing" and "I've got to find my own bag." The greatest psychologist in what is called the *existential* movement is Rollo May, a Madison Avenue psychotherapist. In his book *Love and Will*, he says that everyone has deep needs for creative expression and that one must find some creative outlets if he is to find himself as a person.

The world *person* is from the Latin *persona*, meaning a mask, such as the ancient Roman actors wore in plays. To change roles, they simply changed masks. So a person is an individual with status, one who plays a certain role in society—one who is Somebody. We often think of creativity as limited to the fine arts, but the jobs of a welder and a barber and a housewife are all very creative. And creativity does not require an objective product; rendering a service such as that of a preacher or teacher is creative. It also does not have to make money; it may be a hobby or a cause to believe in and work for.

But in any case it is something that marks our own uniqueness as Somebody. This is what gives the feeling of having something worthwhile in life going for us, so that when the time comes to fight life's battles, we will stand and overcome rather than copping out by some route of escape from reality. Then we will have a meaning and purpose in life that makes the effort worth its cost.

This meaning will involve some task to complete that we feel is worthwhile, but the task will always be "people-oriented"—that is, it will be something that, if successful, will mark us as Somebody in the eyes of someone. We may have nobody in life now, but the unconscious hope is that meeting our goal will attract somebody to us who will really appreciate and care about us. We may even experience this reward in fantasy as one that will occur later, even after our death. But always the real meaning comes from a real or imagined intimate personal relationship, the kind of relationship that is too subtle to define but that is called an "encounter." We will learn more about this later.

Chapter 4

The Logotherapy of Viktor E. Frankl: The Key to Motivation

While the psychology sketched in the previous chapter is nothing new in human history, there is a new voice today who has summed it all up in a fresh and logical form. More than anyone else, he has cut directly to the core of the matter in his analysis of the human condition, of the nature of the underlying psychological need, of the way in which this need gets blocked in modern society, and of the attendant ways in which we cop out from facing the real situation, of which alcohol represents only one. He is Dr. Viktor E. Frankl, a professor of psychiatry at the University of Vienna Medical School. In the present chapter, we will present his system and its principles. They can help you greatly. No matter what theory of the cause of alcoholism you follow, taking that *first* drink is your own responsibility (this is agreed upon by all theories), and therefore problem drinking is a copout from facing life and can be corrected only by the motivation furnished by a real meaning and purpose in life. Frankl's logotherapy can help you gain that motivation.

First, let's look at a typical case I treated by logotherapy, and then we can analyze the underlying principles that operated in it.

Josephine Purvis was twenty-four years old, reared in a professional family, a college graduate, wife of a graduate student in professional training, and the mother of a two-year-old girl. Her early training had been rather strict. She had long-standing feelings of inadequacy and physical inferiority, which related closely to competition with an older, more attractive sister. Actually, Josephine was quite attractive except for some excess weight, which seemed to stem from compulsive and compensatory overeating. She harbored ambivalent hostility toward her sister, her father, and her husband. She felt dependent and believed her own resources were inadequate, but she bitterly resisted her dependency and yearned for a real identity of her own. The results had been repeated flare-ups of marital conflict and periods of depression.

Her need to find a meaning and purpose in life was clearly indicated by such statements as, "I'm trying to prove who I am, and what I want to be. But how do I do it?"

Frankl is careful to point out that logotherapy is no panacea and is not for all patients, and that many cases may be successfully approached from more than one frame of reference. However, it soon became apparent that this was a case that could most readily be interpreted from the point of view of logotherapy. So I proceeded to employ this orientation.

The principal technique of logotherapy is called *dereflection*. This is a process of diverting attention from symptoms (in this case, the patient's feelings of hostility and depression) to that part of personality (her potential) that was intact and unaffected by the illness and was ready to be utilized in finding a meaning and purpose in life. Frustration of this basic need has resulted in the disorder.

The patient was led to analyze and accept her considerable assets, including her achievements—such as attracting and winning a desirable husband and producing a very lovely daughter—which she had ignored or minimized. She was further led to consider the real underlying feelings of worthlessness and inadequacy that had created the sense of meaninglessness, and to think about ways in which she could further turn her assets to the task of meaningful achievements. These would give her life a unity of purpose and a sense of being the Somebody that she wished to be.

In the tenth therapy session she reported: "I've been taking some steps. I've started cooking and have done some painting, and I am real pleased. We are much freer with each other and happier together. I think I've found what I want in life. It sounds corny, but what I really want is a home and children."

At the beginning of therapy, she had discounted these values as life goals and had felt that she needed to find some means of achievement that would make her outstanding among people. Only such accomplishment would, she felt, prove that she was equal to her sister. But she had despaired of attaining this kind of success. Now she was beginning to see this fulfillment in things not only within her potential but also within her present achievement.

She did not make constant progress, however; patients seldom do. At the fifteenth session, she expressed doubts about her goals, although she was sure she did not want to be a career woman as she had earlier thought. By the nineteenth session she had settled down considerably, saying, "I just feel different, as though a weight were lifted from my chest. I'm not as tense with the baby, and many of my former anxieties are gone. And Jack and I are planning for the future."

In the twenty-sixth session, she reported, "The time doesn't drag any more, and I'm no longer bored. I attribute it to being busy and to the fact that we are doing things together. I'm asking myself, what is a woman? Well, a woman is one who is pretty, sexy, and feminine—not necessarily to others, but to herself. And I'm beginning to feel like all of these things. I think I'm much more content."

A few weeks prior to this, she had finally started on the diet she had been postponing for a long time, and she was now sticking to it with good results. She continued improvement both in this and in attitudes of self-confidence and lessened hostility, and she found more and more meaning and contentment in everyday family life—in her husband and baby, and in long-range planning with the family as a focal point.

She was seen for a total of thirty-six sessions, at the conclusion of which the family moved to another community where the husband was to complete his professional training. At time of departure, all was well. Nearly a year later, she returned for a visit and called upon me informally. She reported that everything was fine and proudly displayed a new baby, her second child. It appeared that she had found a place for her life, a true identity and purpose that had given her the feeling of being Somebody. I have seen her several times since then, and, at our last meeting (four years after therapy), she was still doing well.

Basic Concepts of Logotherapy

In order to see what really happened in this case, we must review and summarize the basic concepts of Frankl's logotherapy. Since this therapy is a means of personality development, we will look at Frankl's view of the primary human motive in the shaping of personality.

But first we need a definition of the term *personality*. As mentioned in the previous chapter, the word comes from the Latin *persona,* "mask." In the ancient Roman and Greek plays, the actors portrayed a given character by wearing a distinctive mask. Thus, they could play many roles simply going off stage and changing masks. As the Latin suggests, a person is an individual with a role to play in society, and personality is the sum total of all of the patterns and characteristics of behavior that make up his particular role, or "style of life" as psychiatrist Alfred Adler called it.

Now, there are a number of different views of the dominant factor in personality. In order to understand Frankl's view, let's compare it with some others.

Sigmund Freud, the famous Viennese psychiatrist who founded psychoanalysis around the turn of the century, felt that the basic motive in human personality was the tendency to seek self-satisfaction. This is known as hedonism, or what Freud called the *pleasure principle.* He considered all pleasure to be directly or indirectly rooted in sex, but he interpreted sexual energy much more broadly than we usually do. For example, he believed it included the creative energy spent in building a bridge just as much as that involved in the begetting of children. But for Freud, man was always motivated in one way or another by what might be called the "will to pleasure."

Alfred Adler, another Viennese psychiatrist, was a contemporary of Freud, although younger, and he was also instrumental in the early development of psychoanalysis. Adler departed from Freud in some basic ways, however, and his point of view became known as the "second Viennese school of psychiatry" (the first being that of Freud). Adler, like Freud, felt that all human motivation could be basically traced to one underlying principle, but he differed with Freud as to the nature of this principle. Whereas Freud thought in terms of sex, Adler took his lead from the German philosopher Friedrich Nietzsche and said that man primarily strives to achieve power or mastery over the environment. (Nietzsche believed that only the strong should survive and that the weak should perish, and in this way a super race would be created.)

Whereas Freud had thought that human conflicts result from the failure to keep pleasurable goals in realistic balance (he believed the "reality principle" controls excesses of the "pleasure principle"), Adler said that our difficulties arise when our need for mastery is not properly fulfilled through our other innate need of "social interest." When we do not direct normal mastery needs into socially useful channels, we usually run into conflict and failure. As a consequence, we feel inferior; and Adler gave us the term *inferiority complex* to represent the resultant neurotic state. For him, then, all of man's behavior shows in some way the operation of what might be called the "will to power."

In common with these two views of personality, Viktor Frankl (whose school of thought is sometimes called "the third Viennese school of psychiatry," since he, too, is Viennese) also holds that all of man's behavior is influenced by a unitary principle. He further agrees that we do see in human life a lot of pleasure-seeking and power-seeking behavior. But he holds that these are distortions of the real underlying human need.

The truly universal human urge, he says, is to find a meaning and purpose in life that will furnish one an identity, that will give a person a reason to go on under whatever circumstances he must endure. Frankl loves to quote Nietzsche on this one point, although he has little in common with most of Nietzsche's philosophy, which is usually considered a very pessimistic view of life. Nietzsche did say, however, "He who has a *why* for his life can stand almost any *how*." In other words, a person who has a real reason to live can put up with almost any living conditions. This is Frankl's main point.

Frankl holds that even power-seeking behavior is a method by which one attempts to reach the goal of finding meaning in life: If we can influence others, we can find an identity for ourselves, and we can use the power to achieve a meaningful and purposeful goal. However, if we fail, we then try to drown our pain in temporary immediate pleasures, and thereby we exhibit behavior that fits Freud's concept of personal pleasure as the main human need.

Thus, going beyond Freud's "will to pleasure" and Adler's "will to power," Frankl has set the "will to meaning" as man's primary motive.

All three views are correct to some degree. Man seeks, as the psychologist L. A. Averill put it, to "project the ego." (*Ego*, the Greek word for "I," is Freud's term for the inner core of personality or the "self.") This translates into somewhat the same concept as Adler's mastery need and the "self-actualization" need spoken of by Maslow. And it can also be seen even in Freud's "pleasure principle" when the latter is tempered by the "reality principle" (or by the seeking of realistic, socially efficient goals).

In other words, the basis of human motivation is that we all want to be Somebody, to find a personal identity that will make our lives meaningful and worthwhile. The advantage of Frankl's "will to meaning" is that it points directly to this need and makes more explicit what is actually going on in man's universal struggle. To understand how he arrived at this view of human motivation, we need to take a brief look at his own unique life experiences.

His fascinating story is recorded in his best-selling book, *Man's Search for Meaning.* You would probably enjoy reading this along with the present book. Following it, you would also profit by his *The Doctor and the Soul* and also by Joseph Fabry's *The Pursuit of Meaning*, a popularized version of logotherapy. (See bibliography for these references.)

Viktor E. Frankl was born in 1905 and educated at the University of Vienna, from which he received both an M.D. degree and a Ph.D. degree in philosophy. Before the outbreak of World War II, he had become a neuropsychiatrist. When Hitler entered Austria, Frankl knew that, being Jewish, he was in danger. He had obtained a visa to America for himself, but he could not get visas for his aged parents. For this reason he decided to stay in Vienna.

Later he, his parents and his first wife (whom he had recently married) were incarcerated in the concentration camps. Family members were not allowed to remain together, and Frankl did not know until the end of the war and liberation by the Allies whether any members of his family were still alive. They were not.

When he got back to Vienna and started teaching at the University's medical school, he began to formalize the system of logotherapy, which had been growing in his mind long before the war and which he tested in almost three years in concentration camps. He concluded that it takes one thing to survive under life's most trying circumstances: An unwavering faith that life always has a meaning and purpose and that each person has a job to do right up to the last breath.

We have seen Frankl's "will to meaning" in operation in the case of Josephine Purvis. Now let's look at some more examples.

A prime illustration of this process is that of a well-born Jew who lived in the days when the Hebrews were still under Roman rule. He was a man of position and education, and he enjoyed Roman citizenship and occupied a place of prominence among his people.

This resulted in a special assignment: In order to help maintain the faith of his fathers, he was to aid in stamping out a small, unruly, and threatening cult that was beginning to be a problem to both the Jews and the Romans. Little bands of these cultists were to be found in many of the leading cities—in Antioch, Corinth, Damascus, and others, in addition to the capital, Jerusalem.

This man took to his assignment with enthusiasm and earned quite a reputation for efficiency at the job. After some time, he headed for one of the outlying groups in the distant city of Damascus.

The journey was long and monotonous, and on it he had a lot of time to contemplate this assignment, to think about what it meant. And the more he thought about these little congregations of believers in a new religious approach, the more he remembered their happiness and hope in the face of adversity and suppression.

Here was something that offered a real cause to these people. Something they could believe in with a complete dedication. This belief enabled them to withstand whatever pressures were placed upon them and to come back bravely for more. Not often had he seen such faith. It had given these people something worthwhile to live for, a real sense of mission and identity, a purpose that made the pressures worth withstanding.

The more the traveler thought about this, the more he questioned whether it was right to stamp this movement out. In fact, the followers seemed to have something in life much better than he had to offer.

Then all at once it came to him: the real meaning and purpose in his own life was not in suppressing these groups but in joining them. This realization struck him as a great and blinding flash of light, and from that moment on the light of this new life and its meaning never left him. The new orientation changed his remaining years quite radically; it took him from a life of comfort and security to a piecemeal existence of danger and suffering. In the end, it led to his execution. But never once did he regret the decision to change, for it gave him a dynamic sense of meaning and purpose such as he had never before known.

And so great was the success of his new life on behalf of this struggling little religious sect that now, after nearly two thousand years, he is regarded as one of the most influential figures in history.

His name? No doubt you have already recognized it; he was Saul of Tarsus, who, after the light that changed his life, became Paul the Apostle. And of course the religious sect consisted of the followers of Jesus of Nazareth who came to be called Christians.

Paul always had a why for his life, a cause for which to live, and, when the time came, for which to die. This kind of why for one's life has been found by different people in an endless variety of causes.

Perversions of Will to Meaning

The causes to which people dedicate their lives may be either good or bad in their effect upon society. Adolf Hitler had a cause. Destruction can be as meaningful to some people as construction is to others. The will to meaning often appears in perverted form, and this can result only in frustration, failure, or even grim tragedy. Here are some examples:

Lee Harvey Oswald grew up as a lonely and isolated boy, who, over years of childhood wandering from city to city with his mother, repeatedly tried to find an identity, and equally often felt rejected. He was never really successful at anything, from football to books. Truancy led to a psychiatrist but not to relief from failure. At the earliest opportunity, he joined the marines, but once again he failed to find a place for himself, being court-martialed twice and labeled a misfit.

After returning to civilian life, he studied Russian and went to Russia as a tourist, then sought to defect to the Soviet Union. He was rejected for Soviet citizenship, but was allowed to remain as a resident alien, hold a job, and marry a Russian girl. However, he soon became disillusioned with Russia; again he had failed to find a place. Through the efforts of the State Department, he was allowed to return home with his wife and daughter. He drifted from job to job without finding a challenge. He tried to find his cause in an anti-Castro Cuban organization but again was rejected. Then he tried to return to Russia, but the Russians didn't want him.

He was holding a temporary job at the Texas School Book Depository in Dallas when President John F. Kennedy toured the city on November 22, 1963. The rest is history. At last Lee Harvey Oswald had found a way of being Somebody. If he could not be the best at anything acceptable in society, he would be the worst. His long search for a meaning and purpose in life was over. True, the meaning would be one of infamy in society's terms, but it would point clearly to his deeply frustrated struggle to find satisfaction of the fundamental human urge described by Frankl.

Robert Benjamin Smith, eighteen, was "a kid that nobody knew" in his small home town in Arizona. An introverted loner, he was considered a strange and different boy, although he was never bad. He merely kept to himself and never allowed anyone to get close to him. Even his neighbors in the little Mormon community were hardly aware of him—until November 12, 1966.

On that date, Robert was taken, laughing, by the police from a beauty salon. He had forced seven women and children to lie face down on the floor and then coldly and methodically had shot each in the head. Five of the victims died.

He told police that he had gotten the idea from similar mass killings in Chicago and Austin, Texas, and that he had been planning such a murder for some time. When asked why, he said, "I wanted to get known, to get myself a name." The boy nobody knew had felt a meaningless void; now he had found an identity. And even being somebody society condemned could offer a meaningful release from the intolerable emptiness of being ignored—a perverted fulfillment of the will to meaning.

James B. French, twenty, was serving a life sentence for murder. As a hitchhiker, he had robbed and killed the man who had picked him up. In prison he killed his cellmate, and he was sentenced to die. His attorney gained two new trials, each of which ended in the death sentence. But throughout the proceedings, French waged a long battle from death row to obtain execution. The attorney tried for a new review of the case, but French finally obtained dismissal of the court-appointed attorney and elicited promises from his parents to make no further efforts to save him. He asked the court to uphold the death sentence and hoped for speedy execution.

French had been a mental patient and had been in and out of jails and prisons since he was sixteen. He had never had a purpose for which to live. At last, he found a sense of meaning for his final days—in the cause of obtaining his own death. This unique twist to his case gave him a personal identity that satisfied a long-frustrated will to meaning, even though this satisfaction represented a masochistic or self-punishing perversion.

So how do we select a cause for our own life that makes it worthwhile? Shall it be a "good," or socially constructive, cause or a "bad," or socially destructive, cause? Logotherapy, as a form of existential philosophy, teaches that as human beings we are free to choose for ourselves. No one else can make the choice for us. When we do not readily find a good cause, we may be tempted to adopt a bad one.

Only we can decide. But the decision may be made easier by reflection upon the ends met by the Apostle Paul on the one hand and by Adolf Hitler on the other. Both died for their causes. And both will be long remembered in history. But which way do you want to be remembered?

Of course, most of us won't be remembered either way in the history books. But we will all be remembered by somebody important to us. We have our own private history, and we can find some cause that can make our having lived worthwhile and worth remembering when we are gone. That is, we can find it if we want it badly enough to search. Or we can give up, let life pass through our fingers as meaningless, and end our days in despair. The choice is up to each of us.

Summary of Principles

Now let's return to a summary of the principles of logotherapy, as Frankl presents them in the chapter on his concepts in the second part of *Man's Search for Meaning:*

First and foremost is, of course, the concept of the "will to meaning" as man's primary source of motivation. When one does not find an adequate outlet for this basic need to find meaning and purpose in life, he develops a state of mind that Frankl calls existential vacuum.

Existential vacuum is the experience of a lack of meaning and purpose in one's personal existence, which creates a feeling of empti- ness, manifested primarily by boredom. In other words, when we don't find Nietzsche's *why* for our life, we get tired of putting up with the *how* of it. And when we lack awareness of a cause or purpose that can give us a personal identity as Somebody, we are going to have this feeling. It is not per se a mental or emotional illness; Frankl characterizes it as the human condition of our times. This is so because, in today's computerized and mechanized mass-production world, the individual has largely lost his sense of personal identity and value. Frankl feels that at least 50 percent of the general population experiences at one time or another this condition of existential vacuum.

Existential frustration may occur if the condition of existential vacuum continues over a period of time without relief. Frustration is an emotional response to the blocking of one's motives or patterns of activity to fulfill needs. When we need something badly and fail repeatedly to achieve it, we inevitably become frustrated. If we fail to find a meaning in our personal existence, in time we become existentially frustrated.

In addition to existential frustration, we may also have neurotic or psychotic symptoms. If we have the underlying symptoms of mental or emotional illness and at the same time experience the condition of existential frustration, we then have become the victims of what Frankl describes as a new neurosis: *Nöogenic neurosis.* (*Nöogenic* means "generated by a lack of meaning in life.")

Nöogenic neurosis is, Frankl believes, present in about 20 percent of the patients who come to a mental hygiene clinic for help. Such patients should first be treated for removal of the neurotic symptoms by whatever mode of therapy the practitioner may prefer. But Frankl contends that the mere removal of the pathological symptoms will not alone constitute a cure, for if the condition called existential vacuum is not also relieved, the patient remains basically frustrated in fulfillment of his strongest human need, and in time this emotional conflict will lead to a redevelopment of the same or other neurotic symptoms. Therefore logotherapy is needed following psychotherapy, or perhaps concomitant with it, in order to complete the cure.

There is experimental evidence to support the basic concepts of Frankl's logotherapy. The Purpose-in-Life Test, devised by myself and L. T. Maholick, M.D., is a measure of existential vacuum that has been widely used in doctoral dissertations, master's theses, and other studies, most of which confirm that this fundamental concept of logotherapy is based on fact. In addition, there is a growing body of scientific literature, including papers by Frankl, myself, and others, that lends weight to the validity of logotherapeutic principles.[1]

Now we come to the steps in logotherapeutic technique. As we have seen in the case of Josephine Purvis, logotherapy is a process of guiding a person in finding meaning and purpose or a *why* for his life.

Dereflection is a term Frankl applies to this guidance, the end result of which is the filling of the existential vacuum with a *raison d'être,* or reason for one's personal existence, an identity as Somebody. In dereflection we accept *for the time being* the symptoms as they are, and look beyond them; we "dereflect" attention from the immediate painful situation to unimpaired assets and potential, which can be utilized in spite of the symptoms.

This process implies two basic axiomatic assumptions. We will state them first and then show why they are justified.

1. Finding meaning in life is in the last analysis a spiritual experience.

2. Finding meaning implies that man has a freedom to choose and that his destiny is contingent upon his choices.

Now let's examine the first axiom in more detail.

Finding a meaning and purpose for one's life is a spiritual experience, but this does not necessarily imply that it is religious. In order to understand what is meant here, we need to examine a difficulty in translation of the word *spiritual* from the German, in which Frankl's first two books were written. (Frankl now writes fluently in English, and his last works have been written in this language.)

In German, the noun *Geist* is one of the words for "mind." It refers particularly to the striving, aspirational, and inspirational aspects of mind. From it we get two adjectives, *geistig* and *geistlich,* both of which would be translated in English as "spiritual." The first, however, refers to strictly secular aspects of spirituality, whereas the second is ecclesiastical in reference. Frankl uses the first, but there is no way to indicate the exact meaning of this word in English. For us the word *spiritual* usually has a religious connotation; but it can be used in a much broader sense that might or might not involve religion as we usually think of it, and this broader meaning pertains to logotherapy.

Perhaps these definitions can be made clear by an analogy with some concepts drawn from Alcoholics Anonymous. The first two points of the AA twelve-point program can be paraphrased like this:

1. We admitted that we were powerless to overcome our problem alone.

2. We turned to a Power greater than ourselves as a source of strength.

I have talked with a number of the leaders of the AA movement in several communities, and I gather from what they tell me that *Power* in their terminology has about the same kind of meaning as the word *spiritual* in the frame of reference of logotherapy. That is, AA does not describe this Power in terms of any particular kind of religion or religious concept, but as God in the particular sense in which each AA member conceives of a guiding Power in the universe beyond that of man himself. For some, this might fit a particular theological system or religion, and the term would then refer to God as conceived by that religion. For others it might refer simply to an organizing principle in the universe. But in any case, this principle means that the AA member, in order to be helped, has to look beyond his own strength to a source of meaning that includes man but that is greater than man himself. Thus, he does not have to be religious in the conventional sense, but he must believe in an overall spiritual meaning in human life.

This is essentially what Frankl is getting at when he says that the process of finding meaning and purpose in life is in the last analysis a spiritual experience. In the concluding chapter of *The Will to Meaning,* he notes that logotherapy leaves the door to religion open and leaves it up to the patient whether or not to pass through it. "It is the patient who has to decide whether he interprets responsibleness in terms of being responsible to humanity, society, conscience, or God," he states.[2]

Frankl points out that an animal that is being used in a medical experiment to develop a cure for human disease is not able to grasp the meaning of its suffering, for with its limited intelligence it cannot enter into the world of man, the only world in which its suffering is understandable. Similarly, it is conceivable that there is still another dimension, a world beyond man's world, in which the question of an ultimate meaning of human suffering will find an answer.

Albert Einstein said that to find a satisfactory answer to the question of the meaning of life is to be religious. If we subscribe to his definition of religion, Frankl notes, then man is basically religious in nature, for he seeks an answer to this question.

> People who limit reality to what is tangible and visible and for this reason tend *a priori* to deny the existence of an ultimate being . . . insist that God must be visible. But if they had ever stood on a stage, they could have learned a lesson. Blinded by the footlights and spotlights, a man on stage cannot see the audience. Instead of an audience there is a huge black hole. He cannot see the people who are watching him. And man, standing on the stage of life and playing a role in life, cannot see before whom he is playing the role.[3]

These are some of the reasons why Frankl believes in an ultimate or spiritual meaning and purpose in human life. Speaking for myself, I have got to believe this, too, because I cannot look into the sparkling eyes of a little child and believe that he was created only to live and wither into dust. I cannot feel the tender press of a loved one's kiss and believe that that one is but a momentary flash in the dark sky of a vast cemetery of space. I cannot view the great panorama of human life, with its sorrows and pains, joys and pleasures, and believe that all of these things, good and bad alike, are destined to be swept together into a mass of the matter and force that compose them. I cannot believe this same endless, hopeless cycle is only to be repeated, going on through its valueless, meaningless, unintelligible whirl forever and ever. No, I cannot view all of this without believing in things felt but unseen; for even though their existence is not yet, and may never be, objectively recorded fact, they are almost universal facts of the human heart.

Many of my scientific friends would reproach me with the statement that, as one whose biography appears in *American Men and Women of Science,* I am departing from scientific objectivity and becoming guilty of emotional bias. True, but in turn I would remind them that the rigorous denial of any ultimate meaning and purpose in the universe made by so many of them is an equal bias, except in an opposite direction. Some of us reveal a clear wish to perceive meaning in the universe, while others show evidence of a definite wish to perceive no ultimate meaning. Frankl contends that all of us have a deep need —which he believes is a fundamental human need—to perceive meaning and purpose in human life. We may be conscious of this need and seek to fulfill it. On the other hand, if we fail to find this fulfillment, we may grow unconsciously angry and hostile toward others who seem to have found an ultimate meaning in life while we cannot find one for ourselves.

There are many scientists who, like Einstein, find a faith in ultimate meaning, but there are many more whose training in the rejection of all evidence that is not strictly objective makes it impossible for them to hold such a faith. They usually show as much emotional bias in this rejection of faith as do those whom they accuse of holding faith on emotional rather than rational grounds. Thus, these scientists without faith show evidence of a frustrated will to meaning and a desire to destroy in others what they have been unsuccessful in obtaining for themselves. A former professor of mine once said that if all of the emotional bias were removed from scientific literature, you could write the history of science on a postage stamp.

Several generations ago, Thurlow Weed wrote, "We are not called upon to believe anything more incomprehensible than our own existence. . . . If we are to believe nothing except what we understand, we should go through life incredulous and aimless." The scientist who tries to maintain complete objectivity not only deceives himself in thinking this possible, but also destroys life meaning in the attempt.

So I, like Frankl, must accept this first axiom of logotherapy, that finding meaning and purpose in human life is a spiritual experience—remembering that this term is used in a broad sense, that may include organized religion for some but not for others. If you can accept this axiom on either a religious or a secular basis—and certainly the vast majority of people can—you have passed the first milestone in logotherapy and are ready to consider the second.

Let's examine in more detail that second axiom: finding meaning in life assumes that man is free to make his own choices and, furthermore, that his destiny is contingent upon the choices he makes.

This axiom is derived from the primary tenet of the philosophy known as existentialism. Logotherapy is a psychiatric application of existential philosophy. Therefore, to understand this second axiom, let's take a look at the basic ideas of existentialism.

Existentialism can be thought of as a way of life—that way of life in which the individual accepts that he is free to choose what he will make of his own existence and therefore assumes the responsibility for his own choices. It contrasts with mechanism and determinism, which hold that every aspect of our behavior is fixed by mechanical cause-effect relationships in nature and that, therefore, man can exert no voluntary or independent free will or control over his own destiny, since what each person will become is predetermined, in the last analysis, by circumstances beyond his direction.

The existentialist believes that even though there are consistently repeated happenings in nature (like the experiment of dropping two unequal weights from the Leaning Tower of Pisa and finding that both always reach the ground at the same time), and even though these happenings serve the scientist well in accomplishing his practical aims of building things that make us all more comfortable—man himself can *will* independently of these laws of nature. He can choose to do anything of which he is physically capable, regardless of circumstances that would appear, at first sight, to control his thinking and the way he would want to act in a given situation.

The existentialist does not deny that natural laws are inviolable, but he believes that, in spite of the fact that physical happenings in nature are determined by these set laws, the mind of man is not thus limited. He would agree that many aspects of the mind are controlled by laws as clearly set as those governing the fall of a rock—that heredity and environment place limits upon available choices—but he believes that man's *will* (what the psychologists call volition) can function independently of such laws. One can always choose to strive for any goal, whether or not it is realistically attainable. Of course, one should aim practically, but even in the rare situations where no practical goal can be attained, the choice to strive is important.

Man's Will Is Free

Thus, existentialism makes this fundamental axiomatic assumption that the will of man is free: he can will as he chooses. Now no one can actually prove this either way, so it becomes a matter of each person's faith or of what seems to him to be true from the standpoint of his own total life experience. But existentialism charges every man who will accept this axiom to be always aware of his own freedom to choose what he wills to do in a given situation and of his freedom to struggle to accomplish what he decides upon. Of course, he cannot be guaranteed success in his struggle, but his chances of achieving it are certainly much greater than if he does not try.

Many critics of existentialism have felt that this philosophy does not recognize or accept the great influence of heredity and environment upon all of us, but such is far from the truth. Existentialism not only recognizes these factors but also holds that they do place many limitations upon us through the lack of specific capacities or aptitudes and opportunities necessary to achieve many of the goals we might choose to set for ourselves. It would add, however, that if we are not careful, we will find ourselves using these limitations as excuses not to do our best, because it takes real effort to struggle in the face of opposing odds. We can easily fall into the trap of feeling sorry for ourselves and hating the world for being unfair, rather than trying our best to do as much as we can in spite of our handicaps.

While we cannot prove scientifically whether human volition or will can operate independently of "conditions" or cause-effect antecedents of heredity and environment, we can say that the will is always *phenomenologically* free. That is, the phenomenon or appearance is always one in which we experience the sense of freedom of choice.

To take an example: Suppose you buy a car on Saturday afternoon and give the dealer a check. He refuses it, saying, "How do I know you won't stop payment on this check, draw out all your money, and leave town Monday morning?"

You become indignant. "Listen, my friend, I am A. B. Blank. I have lived and done business in this community twenty years. You know my reputation quite well. You know that my word has always been my bond. You know I would not sacrifice all this for a car."

"Oh, I don't doubt your good intentions," he might return. "Certainly you now intend to honor the check. But in spite of a lifetime of good character, you cannot possibly know all of your secret motives and the hidden influences of heredity and of your past environment, and you cannot know what unforeseen environmental influences await you between now and Monday morning. These influences might force you to will differently then. So, you cannot possibly make any promise which you can be sure that you will even *will* to keep when the time comes. Therefore, I cannot depend on your freedom to *will*, or choose, what you will do, and I do not dare take your check for the car."

Now the truth is that, scientifically, the car dealer is right. There is no way to prove that you can *will* to do or not do something, and even if you can so will, there is no assurance that you are going to maintain even this will to do it, much less the capacity to do it.

But in human experience, it does not appear that way. You might say, "If I gave my word, I would certainly try to keep it. If I changed my mind about wanting to keep it, this would be strictly my own choice. I would be the one to blame if I did not do all in my power to keep my word."

So, your experience is always one of freedom of choice. You feel free. Nobody can prove this freedom scientifically, but if everybody assumed that there is no freedom of the will, what would happen?

The example of the car dealer would be a minor occurrence; we would not be able to conduct the affairs of everyday life. Nobody would dare to plan on anything.

The mechanistic scientists want a predictable world; and therefore they resist the idea of freedom of the will. They say that, if man's will is free, he can act capriciously, and therefore such freedom can have no place in an orderly universe. It is their job to discover this order and to use it to predict and control natural events.

But in actuality, the assumption that there is no freedom leads to the exact opposite of order in human behavior. If we all really felt we were not free to make our own choices of how to face and deal with the conditions set for us by heredity and environment, we would also feel no responsibility for our behavior. And we would be right. We couldn't be blamed for action over which we had no control, so we would make no real effort to act responsibly. We would give free rein to our passions on the grounds that whatever we did was part of the cause-and-effect sequence of events preordained by the conditions.

Instead of orderly human conduct, there would be chaos. In fact, much of the irresponsible antisocial behavior that characterizes our modern society stems from the fact that many people have studied or otherwise absorbed this scientific doctrine of determinism. As a result, they have unconsciously excused their own behavior as well as that of others on the grounds that it is determined by factors beyond control.

It is true that some forms of criminal and other abnormal behavior are rooted in factors beyond the individual's control. But this lack of control is limited; the individual can indeed control parts of this area of behavior.

No one can draw an exact line between controllable and uncontrollable behavior. Therefore, we must accept responsibility for all of our acts. This means that we must accept the feeling of freedom that we naturally have—that we always have unless it has been distorted by the false training that man's behavior is, like that of a rat, all determined and therefore a person has no responsibility for it. We must act as if we were free, even though we can neither prove nor disprove this freedom by the scientific method.

The eminent minister Ralph W. Sockman and the famous geologist Kirtley Mather have pointed out that we always have an area of free choice within which we may exercise our inalienable right to determine what we will make of our lives.

This freedom of choice may be represented in a diagram by a wandering erratic line contained between two straight parallel lines. These parallel lines are our limitations. Within them we can freely choose what attitudes we will take toward them. We may choose to rebel against our conditions and to fight them, but usually we cannot change them. On the other hand, we may choose to accept whatever conditions of life we must face, and to maintain faith that there is an ultimate meaning and purpose in the fact that we have been given these limitations. The latter choice enables us to go on and do the best we can in our situation, and to find an identity as Somebody in the way in which we use our assets and potentials to accomplish all that we can in spite of these handicaps. Many years ago the same idea was suggested by a friend of mine, Porter T. Bennett, a radio and electronics specialist of Dallas, Texas, whose philosophical wisdom apart from his technical field has long influenced my life.

For many problems there are no solutions, but only adjustment to and acceptance of the meaning of these conditions in our life. To illustrate, let us represent our life by a jigsaw puzzle picture that has some missing pieces. We may never find the missing pieces of the puzzle that represents our total life picture. At first, it seems purposeless that these pieces should be missing, and we resent it. But if we notice the total pattern of the missing pieces, we will perceive a new significance: putting all of these areas into relationship (not just our immediate problem area, but all of the missing pieces) creates a pattern that has its own meaning, a meaning we will miss if we don't look for it.

This uniqueness can furnish the *why* Nietzsche said we must have in order to make it possible to bear almost any *how* in life. This pattern, this special meaning of our individual life, is the quality that marks us as Somebody.

But we will never notice this particular significance in the total pattern of our life unless we set out to look for it, unless we have faith that it is there and expect to find it.

So that's what logotherapy is all about—it is the search for the unique meaning and purpose of your own life experiences, the meaning that will reveal your particular job to do that will give you an identity as Somebody.

This job is not a burden: it is rather a privilege that is uniquely yours—your own personal noblesse oblige or "obligation of a nobleman." In feudal times, the nobleman was obligated to take more risks than others because his unique position placed more responsibility upon him. It is your special obligation to use an opportunity that is uniquely yours to accomplish a worthwhile meaning in life that could exist nowhere except in your own special pattern of personal experiences.

But in order to find this meaning, you also have to assume that you have freedom of choice within your limitations and that by exercising this choice you can face these limitations in a meaningful way. If you believe in this freedom as described in existential philosophy—and most people in everyday life assume such a belief without even thinking about it—you are all set to use it in working out a new and meaningful personal identity.

Finding Meaning for Yourself

Now you are ready to examine the means by which logotherapy explores life experiences in search of the unique meaning of one's personal life. We will now describe the areas of search as presented by Frankl. This process of finding meaning is one of exploring all human values for those that fit best with your own unique life experiences and that you can most profitably pursue as a source of meaning.

Here we must understand the difference in the terms 'meaning' and 'value' as used by Frankl. In logotherapy, a 'value' is a culture-wide source of motivation, whereas a 'meaning' is a source of motivation that is effective for a particular individual. For example, patriotism is a concept that motivates large numbers of people in our society as a whole, and we think of it as a social value. But for John Doe as an individual, patriotism may have little or no motivating effect; in other words, it is not for him a meaning.

In the present period, many people are no longer able to find personal meaning in many of the traditional culture-wide values. It is unfortunate, from the standpoint of social survival, that we as a people do not today have a number of clearly stated values that can give us a sense of unity and direction. But this is an age of individuality, and Frankl teaches that only by the process of education and by our acceptance of full responsibility for our personal choices of meaning can we build an integrated personality with a special life task that will give direction and sense of purpose to our own existence.

In order to do this we must explore all of the areas of traditional values and pick those that can have special meaning to us. In this age of individuality, everyone is, in popular jargon, trying to "do his own thing," to "find his own bag."

Because we are not only in many respects different from each other, but also in other respects alike or similar, we will in this process reestablish group or cultural values, in that many of us will find similar meanings and consequently band ourselves together in an effort to fulfill them. But finding the special means that can make our personal existence worthwhile is still an individual process. Although the logotherapist cannot do this for us, he can guide and help us by pointing to and exploring with us the areas of value that have typified man's search for meaning throughout history.

Frankl points out three basic types of human values that we must explore in order to find our own meanings. They are (1) creative values, (2) experiential values, and (3) attitudinal values. Let's look in detail at what he means by each of these.

Creative values

These are the values involved in producing something. The term *production,* as used here, covers a wide variety of functions. It might represent a job—a profession, trade, or business activity. On the other hand, it might involve a hobby, or some cause that you believe is worthwhile and are willing to invest time and effort to advance. Being a housewife, creating a home and family, represents fulfillment of creative values to large numbers of women, while others turn to a career for creative fulfillment. Different people find creative values in different sources, but there is a creative source for everybody except under extreme and unusual circumstances.

The extreme circumstances in which creative fulfillment is not possible are much rarer than you might suppose. For example, if you were paralyzed from the neck down as a result of polio and had to spend most of your time in an iron lung, you might feel that any further creative achievement in life was impossible. If you had been an artist, you would probably assume that there was no hope for any further work of this type. But there is a woman in Florida named Ann Adams who has faced this identical situation and still creates artistically: she paints by holding the brush between her teeth. Her work is lithographed on Christmas and greeting cards, and she still continues to earn her own living by creative work in her chosen field in spite of what would appear to be an utterly impossible handicap.

Consider also the case of Christy Brown. He has been a cerebral palsy victim since birth and is confined to a wheelchair, having full use of only his left foot. He also has a speech impediment that makes him difficult to understand. If we were in this position, we would probably wonder just what we could do creatively. If we wanted to be a writer, and yet could not control our hands to write or our voice for effective dictation, we would likely feel that we might as well give up. But Christy Brown is a successful novelist, typing out his work with his left foot.

So, creative values are often attainable even when we would usually assume that they are out of reach; but in order to utilize our potential to find and develop them, we have to make a systematic search. Now Adler's "will to power," when governed by his "social interest" need, becomes a need to fulfill creative values. Frankl's "will to meaning" goes beyond Adler's thought to the reason why values should be fulfilled in the first place.

Experiential values

These are the values we attain through experiencing the good things of life. For some people this may represent the fine arts, music, literature, art, and the like. For others it may mean going out into the country on a Sunday afternoon and "communing with nature." For still others it may involve going to Lincoln Park in Chicago, Washington Square in New York, Jackson Square in New Orleans, or the Haight-Ashbury district of San Francisco and talking with all kinds of people. Different types of human experience hold value for different types of persons, but anyone can find some type of human experience that is meaningful to him.

Experiential values are helpful to us, even though we may also at the same time be fulfilling creative values very successfully. In the rare circumstances to be described in which creative values are not possible, we may still find meaningful outlets through experiencing the creative work of others. If, for example, Ann Adams and Christy Brown had not found creative outlets in spite of their handicaps, they might still have continued a meaningful life through experiencing the art and literature created by the geniuses of these fields throughout history.

Besides realization of creative and experiential values, there remains one other source of meaning in life: attitudinal values.

Attitudinal values

When everything else fails, and we seem faced with a hopeless situation, we may still make our life meaningful by the attitude we take toward the conditions imposed upon us. Even in the most hopeless situation, we still have freedom of choice as to how we face our fate. We can become angry, resentful, and go into a deep depression of hopelessness and despair. Or we can take the attitude of facing the situation with dignity and courage, in the faith that, as Frankl feels, all life has unconditional meaning and purpose regardless of circumstances, and that we have been given this circumstance as a part of the total meaning of our life. In either case, we will still have to meet the situation, but the first case results in the desperation and despair of meaninglessness, while the second offers hope and courage.

Attitudinal values enabled Frankl to survive nearly three years in Nazi death camps. We have already sketched his experiences there, and we can easily see that, under the desperate conditions of these camps, both creative and experiential values would have been largely impossible to fulfill. Frankl observed that, under these conditions, only those survived who were able, like himself, to maintain the attitude of unconditional faith in the unconditional meaning of all human life in even the most hopeless circumstances. The way in which one faces his fate, the attitude he takes toward it, is often the determining factor in survival. Because Frankl had a faith that there is a meaning in human life that transcends all conditions, he was able to go on where others, who might have made it had they possessed such a faith, gave up.

Few of us are called on to face such desperate conditions in life. But there are some circumstances that may unexpectedly occur and leave us little chance to fulfill creative or experiential values. Here our attitudinal values offer the only hope of meaning and purpose in life. For example, suppose your doctor told you that you had cancer, that it had metastasized (which means that the malignant cells have spread throughout the body, and that surgery is usually hopeless), and that you had only a few weeks at most to live.

Now, you might find in your remaining days fulfillment of some important creative and experiential values. But most likely you would find that this news had caught you short, that you were not prepared to use this final time creatively, and that the anxiety over the approaching end of life would diminish any experiential values you might seek to fulfill. Theoretically, according to existential philosophy, this might be a great opportunity to telescope a lot of the most meaningful experience of your life into a short time. But in practice, without any external help, you probably wouldn't do this; you would probably become deeply depressed, as do most people who face this kind of situation. Then it would be a matter of whether you found, either through your own resources or through external help, a positive attitudinal value in the situation.

The value is always there, and you always have the choice of whether to take a positive or a negative attitude. If you took the positive attitude, you would come out of the depression and use your remaining days constructively, and die in the faith that an unconditional meaning in all human life had enabled you to fulfill your own personal destiny. Or, if you took the negative attitude, you would remain depressed and in hopeless despair. In either case, you would die. But you would have had the choice of two ways to face death.

The operation of attitudinal values under these conditions is well illustrated by one of Frankl's most famous cases, which he used as a teaching case in the University of Vienna Medical School, and which I have paraphrased below:

The patient was an eighty-year-old domestic suffering from a metastasized terminal cancer. Because she knew this meant death, she was deeply depressed. In demonstrating to his medical students the application of logotherapy, Frankl first made the patient question the meaning of her life on the conscious level rather than repressing her doubts.

Having never married, and being without a family or other relatives, she felt extremely lonely and said that she had nothing to show for her life. She had had some meaningful experiences, some high points, but she felt that they were now all for naught.

> PATIENT: I had a good life . . . but now it all ends . . .
>
> FRANKL: But can anyone undo the happiness you've had—can anyone erase it?
>
> PATIENT: No, Doctor, it's true that they cannot.
>
> FRANKL: Can anyone blot out the goodness . . . or the accomplishment . . . or what you have bravely and honestly suffered?
>
> PATIENT: No . . . and I have had so much to suffer, which I thought was God's punishment. . . .
>
> FRANKL: But perhaps God wanted to see how you would stand it? Cannot suffering be also a challenge? Can anyone remove such an achievement and accomplishment from the world?
>
> PATIENT: No, it remains always.
>
> FRANKL: You have made the best of your suffering, and I congratulate you. Your fellow patients have been encouraged by the fact that in spite of your depression you have still been able to go on and they have seldom had an opportunity to witness such an example. [To the medical school class] *Ecce homo!* [The class burst into spontaneous applause.] Your life is a monument which no one can remove from the world, and you can be justly proud.
>
> PATIENT: [Weeping] What you have said, Dr. Frankl, is a consolation and comfort. I have never had a chance to hear anything like this.

Frankl emphasized the facts that, in spite of her depression, she had faced her situation much more courageously than most of the others on the terminal ward, and that the attitude she would now take toward her death could have a deep meaning: it could be the fulfillment of her destiny through her influence on the others—through the courage she could give them to face their own deaths.

She saw the point and reacted favorably to this; she found the attitudinal value that enabled her to live her remaining days in pride and faith, without depression. She had found meaning even in unalterable suffering. When she died a week later, her last words were, "My life is a monument, so Professor Frankl said to the whole audience, my life was not in vain. . . ."[4]

Notice that there are three steps Frankl followed in this therapy:

1. He first made the patient face her real feeling of despair and hopelessness in the present situation.

2. He showed her that her life up to now had *not* been in vain—she had been more successful than she thought. She *had* accomplished things the world could not take from her.

3. He showed her that her *future* life—even the remaining short few days—had a meaning and purpose in a job to be done: the way she faced the end, her attitude, would give courage and meaning to others.

And thus it is with us all: logotherapy teaches that in every circumstance we can find one or more of the three types of human values that give meaning and purpose to this circumstance and enable us to face life with courage and hope.

This, in summary, is the logotherapy of Professor Viktor E. Frankl. It represents (1) a philosophy of life, (2) a theory of personality, and (3) a technique of treatment of emotional problems. Therefore, it touches many aspects of the human scene, and its concepts are important to philosophers, educators, clergymen, mental health specialists, and, most of all, to everyday people. Logoanalysis as later explained in this book is simply a special application of logotherapy.

Chapter 5

Choosing Your View of Life: The First Step in Applying Logotherapy

Logotherapy, a technique for guiding a person in the search for meaning and purpose in life, is the method of choice in helping many problem drinkers. This is so because many drink primarily to escape the boredom and meaninglessness—what Frankl calls the existential vacuum—of a life that has ceased to hold any challenge and that has deteriorated into an abyss of despair through loss of once-held meanings and values.

The *first step* in applying logotherapy is choosing a basic approach to the question of life meaning. Throughout the entire recorded history of the human race there have been two—and only two—basic attitudes of man toward himself. We find these in ancient Egyptian cultures, in Hebrew life at the time of Christ, and in the America of the last part of the twentieth century. And after five thousand years of recorded history, there is no more accurate way of settling the issue of which one is correct, there is no more proof of the validity of either, than there was in the beginning, So you have to make your own evaluation and choose the view that seems most reasonable to you.

Which you choose does make an important difference, because your choice will determine *how* you are going to proceed in the search for life meaning. And it is important that you do make a choice and not try to evade the question, for those who take the latter course—and they include a large segment of the human race—never really find a true meaning and purpose in life. This is because any genuine meaning stems from one or the other of the two views.

Your curiosity is no doubt by this time sufficiently whetted concerning just what the two approaches could be, although you would probably be able to deduce them for yourself if you tried. Here they are:

1. Man is merely a machine, a mechanical device; his biological organism follows the mechanical laws of nature as do all other aspects of nature, and he is nothing more than any other organism—such as a rat or a cat—except that he is more complex. All of nature is the result of chance factors; in spite of the regularities of natural laws, there is no purpose and meaning behind it. Of course this view would logically hold that there is no afterlife or survival of personality after death.

This is the view of so-called positivistic science, the view of "mechanism," the "reductionist" view which holds that all of man's psychological processes can be reduced to physical processes, the view of "determinism," which considers all mental and physical events to be caused or determined by physical antecedents.

This mechanistic view says that there is no intrinsic meaning or purpose in life. Man's only chance for meaningful living is based on what he can devise for himself. He must lift himself by his own bootstraps, because there is no external help for him from any "high Power." Some, including the famous Harvard behaviorist psychologist B. F. Skinner, would even deny that man can do anything for himself, since, they believe, life is entirely determined by external forces.

The mechanistic view of man is in many respects illustrated by the philosophy of the famous French existentialist Jean-Paul Sartre.

Sartre is the leader of atheistic existentialism. Existentialism, which also has a theistic branch, holds that the focus of the study of man should be on his existence as a human being. And both branches hold that human life cannot be understood by reason alone, and that man has freedom of choice as to how he will face life.

But Sartre believes that there is no meaning and purpose in the universe other than what each human individual can put there for himself. All life is *absurd* (a technical term in existentialism that means, not that life is ridiculous, but that it cannot be comprehended by reason). We are all doomed to defeat in the end, according to Sartre, for there is no justice in nature. But in spite of this, we can each find some values in which we believe, and we can live by these values to the last. And living thus—superimposing our own meanings on a meaningless world—enables us to be superior to the absurdity of it all and to die with dignity in the knowledge that we created our own meaning where there really is none. All of this makes life worth living, as Sartre sees it.

Yes, this is the world of Jean-Paul Sartre, and positivistic scientists have a similar view, although they differ on such matters as freedom of the will and deny the existence of freedom. This is the world of most behavioral scientists today, especially most psychologists. The majority of psychologists consider themselves behaviorists, holding that only behavior, and not subjective experience (or conscious experience), is admissable "evidence" in the study of man.

This is one of the two basic views of nature. It is the majority view in scientific circles today, but it is as old as the hills; it is not something new from the modern laboratory.

There is another view, which also has always been with us:

2. Man is a machine, but he is also infinitely more than a machine. His psychological processes, conscious experience, emotions, and feelings do involve processes in the brain and in the rest of the nervous system and the body, but they cannot be reduced to bodily processes.

Man is more than a biological organism—he is a unique being set apart in nature from all other beings. As the philosopher Max Scheler has noted, he has one capacity not shared by any other of the creatures of Earth: the capacity to contemplate the possible. Only man can see, not merely what is, but what can and should be. The dog accepts nature as is and has no concept of a better world; but man can conceive of a whole new way of life and can work toward its attainment. Man is not limited by the past or even the present; he can control his future.

This view holds that the universe is not merely the product of chance but is designed by an Intelligence greater than that of man. It considers man as a part of this design and therefore believes that man has his own unique meaning and purpose.

And if this is true of man as a species, it is also true of each man and woman as an individual. We all have a destiny to fulfill, a life purpose to carry out.

Each of us must search for it; but when we become convinced that we have discovered it, we have a real mission to fulfill, a cause to work for, a task to complete in life that will motivate us to such a powerful degree that we can go on. We will continue in spite of life's frustrations and make it through or over or under or around obstacles because we have a reason that makes it all worth the struggle.

This view would logically hold that there is some sort of afterlife or persistence of personality after bodily death, although there are those who embrace the view without believing in survival. This nonmechanistic orientation rejects determinism and holds that we are all free within the limits set by heredity and environment to choose how we will face our situation. As Frankl says, life conditions are given to us; how we face them is freely chosen by us.

This is the world of the religious person, but it is also the world of many who do not think of themselves as religious—of many who would certainly not be religious in the institutional sense, in the sense of organized religion, in the "church" sense, but who do believe in a Power greater than man, and who have their own personal ways of contacting this Power. Alcoholics Anonymous is based on this approach, in which each individual defines his own concept of this Power but still turns to it for help.

This is the world of those who believe that there is a Power toward which man can turn for help, whether he does it by religion in the conventional sense or by his own methods. It is a world of purpose and design in which each individual life counts, in which we make our lives count in spite of whatever setbacks and tragedies and frustrations we face. We do this by looking for the hidden meaning in it all, for the way in which all of our life events fit into a pattern and point to a purpose we can fulfill, to a meaning we would not have been able to realize if these problems had not occurred.

This is the *attitudinal value* in logotherapy, described in the last chapter and illustrated by the case of the eighty-year-old woman with terminal cancer, whom Frankl treated. The attitudinal value can be applied by those who follow the mechanistic view of man, by their asking themselves what they can do to turn their rotten luck into some advantage; but it is much more easily applied by nonmechanistic believers in an intrinsic purpose in all of nature, for they do not have to consider their conditions as "rotten luck." They rather think of these conditions as part of a purpose that is to be discovered and fulfilled.

This second, nonmechanistic view of man is called the "teleological" view by philosophers (from the Greek *teleos,* "aim, goal or end"), for it holds that there is a distant plan or design in nature toward which natural events are moving. For most people this view is not only a more optimistic attitude toward life, but also a helpful and needed source of courage when the going in life gets tough. Most people's teeth are not sharp enough and their fingernails are not long enough to go it alone in the human jungle that they often find themselves facing. But for some, like Jean-Paul Sartre and psychologist-sexologist Albert Ellis, this attitude represents a failure of the individual to take responsibility for life upon his own shoulders and to handle this situation without "magical" help (which these authorities believe does not exist in the first place, and which they say they do not want in the second place).

Well, which of the two views of man is right? The truth is that leading spokesmen for both points of view agree that neither view can be proven in the scientific sense. Both are in the last analysis a matter of faith. Many religious persons have a deep and abiding faith that there is a Creator who has a specific plan for their lives. Many like Sartre have a faith that there is not. Sartre says that he intuitively knows there is no God, just as Billy Graham would say that he intuitively knows there is one.

All of this leads many to try to avoid the issue altogether until they reach some life crisis when they need to come to grips with it and to have a faith upon which they can base action. The trouble with such procrastination is that, if you wait until you need a faith, you won't be able to establish it overnight. Whichever way your faith may turn, it has to jell and become a genuine part of you. And until you have a firm decision that fits your personal needs, you won't have real peace of mind.

People are emotionally different in their needs to believe in these two views of the nature of man. You will be able to find a real meaning and purpose in life from either view *if* (1) you *really* believe in it, and (2) you are *emotionally suited* to believe in and to accept this view. The latter factor hangs many people up today. They are trying in this increasingly secular society to believe in, or to live as if they believed in, the mechanistic view that there is no purposeful design in the universe placed there by some Creator. They consider the teleological view mystical, supernatural, and fairy-tale-like, and they want no part of it—until they meet a life situation in which they discover that they are not the superstrong stainless steel independent types they thought they were, and that they really do need some help. Then it is too late to get the help, because their doubts of a purposeful universe have become so firmly ingrained that they cannot readily reperceive the world in meaningful terms.

This point is well illustrated by a patient I had in one of my logotherapy groups in an alcoholic rehabilitation program several years ago. Believe it or not, he was a large-city psychiatrist. When we came to study the present topic, he was deeply moved.

"Doctor," he said, "I am here in the hospital because I cannot resolve this problem in my own mind. I know that's why I drink. I have the emotional need to believe that there is a meaning and purpose in the universe, put there by a Creator who cares about me and will help me fulfill that purpose if I turn to him and seek to find it. But when I try, I am beset with doubts, and I can't stick to either view. I tolerate it as long as I can, and then I grab a bottle."

"Doctor," I returned, "you are not alone in this struggle. There is no proof, but there *is* a lot of evidence. There is evidence on both sides, and each side is convincing to many people who are suited for it. If you will really take the time and energy to search for the evidence on the side you need to believe in, you will find it. And only then will you find yourself."

He went through a long struggle that discouraged him, and he left the hospital without finding himself. But within a year, he had come to grips with the question well enough to get back into practice. When he finds others fighting this battle, he will know how they feel and will probably be better able to help than would a psychiatrist to whom the problem has no personal significance.

For those like him who need to believe in a Higher Power but haven't found satisfactory evidence, the following facts may help:

1. Scientists are losing their sense of intellectual superiority, according to Richard Olson of the University of California at Santa Cruz, writing in *Psychology Today,* January 1976. He notes that certain developments within the sciences, such as the Heisenberg Indeterminacy or Uncertainty Principle, have indicated that there are some physical events that cannot be predicted by natural laws. This leaves the whole field of science vulnerable to critics who have always said that science could never attain absolute knowledge, as noted in the "Press Digest" of *Current Contents* for April 5, 1976. All of which opens the door to the belief that there are some things that cannot be explained by the concept of a mechanistic universe devoid of purpose and design.

2. Elizabeth Kübler-Ross, M.D., whose book *On Death and Dying* (1969) is perhaps the best-known work concerning the terminally ill, has for many years been collecting reports of a large number of individuals who were pronounced medically dead but who later were resuscitated, and who retained memories of this period during which they were supposedly dead. *Reader's Digest* (August 1976) reports interviews with Dr. Kübler-Ross for *Family Circle* and *People* magazines, in which she talked of her conclusions from her studies. She had before then doubted there is any life after death, but changed her mind firmly afterward. She feels that something significant happens within minutes after "clinical" death, as her patients became amazingly peaceful in expression at that time.

Kübler-Ross investigated scores of patients, both religious and non-religious, some of whom had been "dead" for three to twelve hours. Most reported one basic type of experience: they felt as if they had shed their physical bodies, and they experienced peace, freedom from pain and anxiety, and a sense of completeness or perfection. Some could "see" the efforts to revive them, and they resented attempts to return them to a life of suffering. None were afraid to die again.

In February 1977, it was my privilege to participate in a Festival of Meaning honoring Dr. Viktor Frankl, the founder of logotherapy, organized by Dr. Robert Leslie of the Pacific School of Religion in Berkeley, California, upon the occasion of the establishment there of the Frankl Library and Memorabilia. At a dinner for Dr. Frankl, the famous Viennese psychiatrist mentioned that Dr. Kübler-Ross had recently come to see him. I asked him how he had reacted to her collection of cases. He pointed out that, because the concepts of time and space are human psychological constructs and have meaning only in the world of human experience, it is really not valid to think in terms of events after death or before life. This means that, in a sense apart from the human experience of the sequence of events which we consider as time and of the distances which we know as space, the concepts of past, present and future blend, and the meanings of "here" versus "there" merge. Thus life becomes a continuous process (even though it changes in form of expression) without beginning or end. Following the evidence produced by Kübler-Ross, and the reminder of the relative nature of the time-space continua noted by Frankl, one might conclude that it is a basic mistake on man's part to interpret birth-life-death sequences in terms of beginning and end; they are rather episodes in universal experience that transcends time and space. Frankl holds that no experience, once it occurs, can ever be lost—it remains always as an occurrence in nature regardless of all other events that may transpire. (See Frankl's new book, *The Unheard Cry for Meaning: Psychotherapy and Humanism,* New York: Simon and Schuster, 1978; specifically the chapter, "Temporality and Mortality.")

The sum of these facts suggests that life cannot be adequately viewed as an accidental flash in a meaningless universe of absurdity and chaos, but that it is part of a continuing, dynamic, unfolding process. And how can such a process, which is by definition not "chance determined" and chaotic, occur without some kind of Power or Intelligence in the universe to determine or ordain it?

As Martin Heidegger, the great German existentialist philospher, has said, "The existential question [the question of the meaning of existence] is not, Why is this or that here? The real existential question is, Why is there something instead of nothing at all?"

Winston Churchill said to the United States Congress on December 26, 1941, shortly after America's entry into World War II, "I will say that any man must have a blind soul who cannot see that some great purpose and design is being worked out here below." Eugene A. Cernan, Apollo 17 astronaut, said *(The Plain Truth,* June 1976), "When you get out there a quarter of a million miles from home, you look at Earth with a little different perspective. . . . The Earth looks so perfect. There are no strings to hold it up. . . . You think of the infinity of space and time. I didn't see God but I am convinced of God by the order out in space. I know it didn't happen by accident."

3. The biggest barrier to belief in a High Power for many is the sense of thwarted justice that seems to pervade human life. If there were a Higher Power, why would He (or It—or She, in deference to Women's Lib) permit such horrendous circumstances to occur? And when they occur to us, our natural first reaction is, Why me? The answer to this question is crucial in our capacity to find any real meaning and purpose in our lives.

Those whose answer is, It is my rotten luck—the result of "pure chance" in a meaningless universe—must then, in order to find any personal life meaning in this meaningless world, ask themselves the further questions: What can I do on my own, lifting myself by my own bootstraps, since there in no external help, to turn my misfortunes to my own advantage? How can I use them constructively to create a meaning where none now seems to exist in nature? Persons who reason thus must accept responsibility to create such a meaning or perish in despair.

On the other hand, those whose answer to the first question is, These misfortunes and injustices do not seem to make any sense, but I accept them as a part of a plan or design in nature, as a part of the design for my own life, as having a purpose that I cannot see, even though it appears so horribly unjust—those whose answer is along these lines must next ask themselves, What could this purpose be?

Now their third question will be the same as that of those who believe the universe is meaningless and the result of pure chance: What can I now do to use my misfortunes constructively, to turn my suffering to advantage by finding something worthwhile to do that I could not have done so well if these tragedies had not occurred? You may wonder, therefore, what difference it makes whether we believe the universe is chaotic or designed. But there is a big difference here: The "design people" don't have to say, What rotten breaks, but I'll lift myself by my own bootstraps and go on anyway, even though it is very hard to keep up courage in such a terrible world. They instead say, My experiences have been terrible, but they have a purpose that I am supposed to fulfill through having had them; therefore I will search for this purpose, I will try to see what these experiences could be intended to teach me or in what direction they could be leading me. I will choose the positive attitude that such purpose exists, and I will search for it. And in the search I can expect help: I do not have to depend solely on my own strength in a world that is too much for any man; I can look to this Higher Power that has ordained the purpose I cannot see, and I can expect guidance in the search and assistance when I falter.

A strong point regarding this matter of dealing with a frustrated sense of justice in an unjust world is often made by Frankl: he asks, Do you suppose that an animal in a laboratory experiment can understand the meaning of its suffering? Can it comprehend the fact that this unpleasantness serves a purpose higher than any that its limitations permit it to grasp? In the same way, is it not possible that man experiences suffering that has a purpose higher than any that his own limitations permit him to see?

In this connection, an incident in my own experience may illustrate what Frankl is talking about, as he deals with this difficulty most people have in maintaining faith and courage in the face of the ubiquitous occurrence of grossly unjust and unexpected human suffering. One evening I had just returned from church, where the preacher's homily had included the statement that, when he was in seminary, his brother, who was also expecting to become a priest, drowned. His first reaction to the tragedy was to withdraw from seminary. Why should he serve such an unjust God? Fortunately his mother's influence in facing the situation with courage and faith finally turned his own tide and enabled him to go on.

As I returned home with this sermon in mind, I had to step over a freshly painted doorstep to enter our condominium. Our next-door neighbor was outside, and I was suddenly greeted by her dog, whom I had often petted. But now I had to halt the dog's advance upon the fresh paint by a sharp rejecting attitude. The neighbor, seeing what was happening, cuffed the dog sharply, and he yelped in retreat.

I wondered how the dog would react to me when I next saw him, how he would make sense of the fact that one day I petted him and the next rejected him for no apparent reason, and then after that attemped to pet him again. How do you explain to a dog that it was necessary to hurt him in order to prevent greater injury (in this case, getting his paws full of poisonous lead paint, which he undoubtedly would have tried to lick off; as well as his unknowingly injuring others through ruining the paint job)?

How do you explain to a dog the reason for events that are beyond his world of experience and therefore his comprehension? How does God explain to a man?

No, the dog didn't understand; but when I next saw him, he wagged his tail in friendship. He had accepted me on faith, based on the good experiences of the past and in spite of the bad. He wasn't bitter about what he couldn't comprehend. Sometimes dogs are smarter than people.

4. The question of whether the universe is designed and purposeful and of whether there is a Higher Power that made it so are related, as we have seen, to the question of personal survival after death. The latter issue may be better understood by consideration of the fact that personal survival *before* death does not actually occur. That is to say, we do not maintain the same identity throughout life, even though there is a degree of continuity.

This concept is well known in the metamorphosis of some insects, wherein, for example, a caterpillar changes into a moth; but we usually do not associate such a process with human life. And yet in the human organism an analogous process does take place. As we grow from infancy to childhood to adulthood to old age, we go through both physical and mental stages between which there is a thread of continuity based on remembered experience and habits of behavior, but which are separated by differences in appearance, thinking, and behavior that are really more distinct from each other than the differences between individuals at a given period of life. If you are over forty, you are in many respects more like your contemporary friends than you are like yourself at the age of eighteen.

Thus we do not survive this life unchanged; we do not really survive as the same person. We can therefore hardly expect to survive the transition of death unchanged, though the latter may be seen as a *sudden* transition in comparison with the *slow* transition from youth to old age. But here again, since time and space are concepts based on the experience of this life, experience apart from it may not reflect this same sense of time difference. Survival may therefore occur without involving the rigid continuation of form and matter in the frame of reference of time and space to which we are accustomed. And this survival may be based on purpose and design in a meaningful universe, in which we can look to a Higher Power for guidance and help.

5. Evidence that the universe is not a mere mechanism as conceived by materialistic science, but that there are "nonmechanistic" laws yet unknown in nature (which open the door for the concepts of design and purpose in the universe, and for the existence of a Higher Intelligence) is abundant in the field of *parapsychology.* Formerly called psychic phenomena, the occurrences studied in this field include psychokinesis ("mind-over-matter" manifestations), appearances and disappearances that seem to defy the known laws of natural science, mental telepathy and clairvoyance (named ESP or extrasensory perception by Dr. J. B. Rhine at Duke University), and various other related effects.

They are now known as *psi* phenomena. Although many skeptics still exist, the study of these phenomena has considerable scientific acceptance today, as witnessed by the fact that there is a division of parapsychology in the American Association for the Advancement of

Science, whereas parapsychologists could not have gotten through the *back* door of this august body a generation ago.

It is true that the parapsychologists (so called because the "orthodox" psychologists considered them outside of respectable psychology in the early years: Greek *para* means beyond, outside) have not yet produced a truly "repeatable" laboratory experiment. This means one that can be duplicated in virtually any scientific laboratory at will with essentially the same results; and I personally hold out for this criterion as essential, because it has been a cornerstone of proof in all *experimental* sciences. But the evidence for psi phenomena has continually grown stronger over the last forty years.

There is voluminous literature on the subject, which you may find at any good library. The laboratory work is essential to proof, but it grows out of the vast background of frequently reported human experiences that seem to involve such phenomena. I have recorded some of these occurrences in Chapter 3 of my book, *Everything to Gain: A Guide to Self-Fulfillment through Logoanalysis* (see Bibliography). I will give only two examples here, since you can find an abundance of them in literature. In fact, you very well may have some such experience to add yourself; and if you do not, the chances are excellent that someone close to you does have.

A lady told me this story:

"The strangest event of my life occurred on the evening of February 23, 1965. I kept saying that it was not my voice, and yet it had to be. There was no one else around except my escort, who was standing just behind me, ready to open the car door. 'Did you say that?' he asked. 'Did you say, "Don't go down Averill Street"? It didn't sound like you.' 'I—I don't know—it wasn't my voice,' I faltered.

"Actually Averill Street was the closest route to my home from the supper club where we had just finished a quiet meal. At the time I had just begun to recover from a very serious illness and had not been out of the house for two months. My friends had all tried to help in the recovery, and Sam, my escort, whom I had known only as a good friend of my late husband's, took me out for an evening of 'real food and fine music for a change.'

"I had gone against my better judgment, because I had felt apprehensive for no apparent reason. As we now pulled out of the parking lot, Sam said, 'Teresa, I see no reason why we can't go down Averill Street. Do you know of any reason why we shouldn't?' 'No,' I replied, 'I don't know why I said that. It's not my nature to back-seat drive. It just didn't seem like I said it, but I must have. No, Sam, of course there is no reason why we can't go down Averill Street.'

"So we went down Averill. And only several minutes later we were hit broadside on my side of the car by another automobile. The car was totaled, and I suffered a crushed side and permanent nerve damage to my right arm. Sam was not injured.

"When he was allowed to see me in the hospital, his first words were, 'How in the hell did you know we should not have gone down Averill Street?' 'I don't know,' I managed to mumble. 'It just wasn't my voice. And don't blame yourself, because I was warned, and I disregarded the warning.' Even today, on the occasions when my right arm gives me fits, I think back to that strange occurrence and wonder what really happened."

What do you think happened?

The same lady very recently told me another story:

"The air was cold and damp this morning [December 1976], and I wore a head scarf as I drove alone to church, even though head gear is seldom necessary here on the Gulf Coast. As I approached to within two blocks of the church, it felt as though someone in the back seat behind me had suddenly plucked the scarf off of my head. I looked around as best I could while driving, and of course there was no one else in the car, and I could not see the scarf. All of the doors and windows were tightly closed because of the cold weather.

"When I parked the car I began to search for the scarf, but it was nowhere to be found. Thinking it might fall out as I opened the door, I watched closely, and then I searched all around the car and thoroughly in the back, under the seats, and everywhere, but nothing!"

The following morning the lady had her husband vacuum the car and make a thorough search, but nothing was found.

"I simply couldn't believe it," she said, "but my sense of humor finally came through, and I said to myself, 'If I'd known the spooks needed a scarf so badly, I'd have worn a brand new one, and not my old favorite.' "

Well, what do you think happened in this case? Is the lady lying? Are these events hoaxes? Coincidences? Hallucinations? Is the lady crazy?

I don't think so. You will understand why when I tell you that she is my wife. I might also add that my wife, Teresa Croteau-Crumbaugh, is an internationally known handwriting expert, but that she has never shown any special interest in parapsychology, spiritualism, mysticism, or any form of the occult. She is a devout believer in institutional religion, and she has always accepted the existence of a world beyond man's understanding on the basis of a firm but uncomplicated faith, without attempts to rationalize it or to probe its nature. She has never been known to center her thoughts on manifestations of the nonmaterial world, because she has never needed these to bolster her faith.

These manifestations are, however, very abundant in the literature of parapsychology. Now if you are a hard-core mechanist, you will assume such things are impossible, and that people who report them must be lying, crazy, self-deceived, the victims of hoax or coincidence. If you have already determined not to believe, no amount of evidence—not even that of your own eyes—will convince you. But if you have an open mind, you will do a lot of wondering about reports of this type.

And you may find in parapsychology what you need as a basis for a reasonable faith that there is more to the universe than mechanistic science allows. Here you may gain encouraging evidence that there is, after all, some sort of purpose and design in nature and that back of it exists a designing Power.

6.   In conceiving the question of design in the universe, it may help to draw an analogy between what you have to do in interpreting this universe and what you do in perceiving the ambiguous stimuli provided by "projective techniques" in clinical psychology. The best known of these techniques is the Rorschach Ink Blot Test, a series of ten supposedly meaningless ink blots which are variously seen by different people as everything and as nothing under the canopy of heaven. Your personal interpretation will depend upon your unique background of individual experience, although there are common patterns or "popular responses."

Now are these blots the result of "pure chance" or of purpose and design? From one standpoint, they are pure chance, since they were made by pouring ink upon paper with a middle crease and then folding the paper upon the crease and thus smearing the ink. But on the other hand, Hermann Rorschach, the Swiss psychiatrist who invented them, made some ten thousand blots before he got a final ten that elicit the maximal number and variety of responses. So from another standpoint, the blots represent an element of purpose and design superimposed upon the pure chance factors that shaped them.

The late great philosopher Alfred North Whitehead believed that something like this occurs in the world of nature: most events are determined by chance; but every so often, at key points (which Whitehead called "occasions") in a persons's life, nonchance factors—the result of purpose and design put there by a Higher Power—do occur.

From this point of view, the universe is sometimes mechanistic and chance determined and sometimes teleological and purposive. To represent a similar kind of comparison, the philosopher Herbert Spencer used an analogy with a curved lens or mirror: from one side it is concave, from the other it is convex. Both interpretations are true, depending upon the viewing position.

From this analogy, it might seem that we could "straddle the fence" by accepting both views of the nature of the world and of man, and thus avoid a choice or decision between them. But here it should be noted that, in order to use the mirror, we must decide the effect we want, for the image is different from each point of view. So we really do have to decide what we think about life before we can find a meaning in it.

7. In the last analysis, the strongest line of evidence as to whether there is a Higher Power comes from our individual personal experience. This is always the most convincing argument. Dr. Martial Boudreaux, a psychiatrist whom I shall be quoting presently in connection with evidence for the mechanistic view of the universe, says that he has no religious sentiments, but that the nearest thing to them for him is the moving response he sometimes has to music. This shows that he has correctly identified religion as a personal emotional experience, although he has shut off such experience in his own life.

A psychologist friend of mine, who had been religious and then lost her religious faith, told me that she missed nothing about religion except a sense of Presence—the feeling that someone was always with her, which she had once had. This indicates that religion is not social but personal in essence; and belief in the existence of this sense of Presence or Higher Power is determined, not by reason, but by factors of personal experience, which are primarily related to feelings and emotions.

So the best indicator of what your own position should be on this issue is not your head but your heart. If you have the heart for either of the two views, you will put your head to work in finding supportive evidence for it. And there is plenty for each view, although, as we have said, there is no proof of either.

For me, the choice has to be a strong commitment to belief in the existence of this Higher Power, and of intrinsic meaning and purpose in a teleological world. My emotional needs and personal experience in this direction can be shown by an episode in my life some years ago:

Shortly after coming to a new job in a strange community, where I had only a few casual co-worker friends, I had to undergo surgery. The nurse who prepared me for the operation asked, "Who is here with you?"

"What do you mean?"

"Usually when people are operated on, they have a friend or relative who waits outside of the recovery room to see whether or not they make it. Who is waiting for you?"

"Me? Nobody. I've got nobody. I'm here alone."

"Oh. . . . Well, you'll probably make it okay."

One can feel awfully alone at a time like that. Unless you've been there, you don't know how alone.

While I was being prepared, I had a lot of time to feel that isolation, and it can be frightening. I thought of the others around me with families who cared, and I longed for a comforting hand.

And then it was as if there were an unseen Presence with me, and I remembered that I did have Someone, Someone after all—Someone whom I had forgotten, but who had not forgotten me. Yes, there really was help when you were not strong enough to go it alone.

I had long been a believer in this Power. Though I have never been considered a pious person, most have regarded me as religious, and I have thus regarded myself. I have long maintained connections with institutional religion, and I regard this as right for me, though I have been aware that it is not for everybody, not even for all who are religious.

Frankl feels that religion will become more personalized and less institutionalized, even though he does not foresee the collapse of institutional religion. I am personally little concerned with theology per se, but very concerned with the feeling side of religion. And for me, institutionalism helps greatly to maintain and nourish religious feelings. For many others, it serves in an opposite way, to destroy the feelings.

So we each must find our own approach to life meaning, and then—if it involves religion—we must find our own best form of expression of this phenomenon.

I felt I had found a form that sustained me in this operation when I was having difficulty in sustaining myself. Would I have still made it if my belief had been that there is no meaning and purpose, no design, in the universe—that there is no Higher Power upon whom I could rely for help? Probably. But it would undoubtedly have been much harder and more unpleasant.

And of course I might be wrong in thinking I would have made it at all. The depression that grows from intense feeling of loneliness and alienation certainly would not have contributed to recovery; and it might, indeed, have reduced the body's healing capacities by a fatal amount.

All of which reflects the point being herein made, that the really convincing evidence of the existence of a Higher Power comes, for those who find it, from within rather than from without: it stems from personal experience. There are many, even clergymen, who have never had personal experiences that yield a sense of the presence of this Power, but who believe it is there. For many others, only this personal type of experience is convincing.

Now what about the other side of the coin? What lines of evidence are there for those who do not experience a need to believe in this Power, who really show no emotional need for it, and who prefer, like Jean-Paul Sartre, to go through life alone without expecting any outside help? What evidence is there that there is *not* such a Power?

The truth is that, since there is no universal negative, and the existence of such a Power can never be scientifically disproven any more than it can be proven, the negative evidence is, as we have seen, also a matter of faith. But what facts support this kind of faith?

Actually this negative view is based primarily on the assumption that, if there were such a Power, it would be possible to demonstrate the fact scientifically—an assumption that cannot be supported in logic any more than the assumption that the absence of such a Power should be provable scientifically. So one must choose his direction here on the basis of which way his life experience leads him.

This fact is well illustrated through the opinions expressed by a colleague of mine, Dr. Martial Boudreaux, a psychiatrist upon whose ward staff I serve as clinical psychologist. I distributed a questionnaire aimed at eliciting opinions on both sides of the issue of whether there is intrinsic design and purpose in the universe, and I asked respondents to indicate the arguments that were most convincing to them in support of their personal views.

I found that few would take the time to do the questionnaire; and some who did offered either evidence that had little substance or evidence that was entirely too abstract and complicated to help most people who are searching for answers. But Dr. Boudreaux cut quickly and briefly to the core of the issue; and I felt that his views—which are strictly mechanistic and support the position that no Higher Power exists—would serve better than any other material I have come across to represent this orientation. Here is what he said:

> 'I opt for the mechanistic or chance viewpoint. The nature of basic physical and chemical organization determines the future over eons of time. How this basic organization came about or if it is universal I have no idea, and could not care less.... My evidence is based on the sum total of my experience, and it represents the way I have thought since early youth. It includes the sum total of all of my reading and personal conversations with people of all types. I do not consider either view capable of proof, and I do not find this disconcerting. So you take your choice and go with it. Years ago arguments mattered to me; now I don't care. Both sides are incapable of proof, and both are capable of some refutation.... As far as the need for a meaning and purpose in the universe is concerned, I can hack it successfully without one. But each person has to have his own way and to go with it.'

I think there is little that can be added to these statements in representation of the basic mechanistic orientation toward human life. While a large number of people, especially those who are strongly religious on the one hand or strongly antireligious on the other, become quite emotionally biased in their arguments, this psychiatrist has maintained an objective attitude toward both views while choosing one attitude for himself. And that is all we can ask of ourselves or of anyone else.

The key to making a personal decision concerning which of these two basic philosophies of life to adopt lies in one's level of personal self-confidence. If you are self-confident, you will trust your ability to make the right decision. Knowing you can't prove either and that the choice must be made on faith, you will—if you lack faith in yourself—also lack faith in your choice. On the other hand, believing in yourself will mean that you will believe in your choice, even though it is made in the face of incomplete data. To have faith in anything, we must first have faith in ourselves. That is why we will be dealing with ways to build self-confidence in the next chapter.

Chapter 6

Building Self-Confidence and Creative Thinking: The Second and Third Steps in Finding Meaning in Life (Applied Logotherapy)

The *second step* in finding a life meaning is to build self-confidence—belief in yourself and in your ability to arrive at the answers you seek. And the *third step* is related to the second as a natural sequence: if you believe in your abilities, you are ready to use them; and using them to find answers to life questions requires that you think creatively. So once we decide which general approach to life we are going to take, which is like deciding whether we are aiming for the North or the South Pole, we must then ensure our ability to get there by building self-assurance, self-esteem and self-confidence (the *second step*), and then by stimulating our creative processes (the *third step*).

These second and third steps we can take by an exercise that is divided into two parts aimed at these goals. It is short and easy to do, but it will work only if you work at it *regularly*. Nothing will work if you don't do your part.

I call it the Power of Freedom Exercise because it is based on the fundamental assumption of logotherapy (and of all existential thinkers) that man does have an area of free will, that all human life is *not* completely determined by conditioning plus heredity, and that therefore we can exercise some free choices to modify our own situation and to direct our lives toward chosen goals. This fundamental belief in freedom, which has been more fully discussed in chapter 4 on the principles of logotherapy, is essential to our building self-confidence and to developing creative thinking—indeed, to the entire process of finding life meaning.

You may have "bought" this viewpoint by this time. In case you haven't, there is still further evidence we can offer.

B. F. Skinner, the famous Harvard psychologist, believes that we have no freedom of the will, that we are only pawns pushed about by influences of heredity and environment, and that our behavior is all conditioned by external forces—like the behavior of the rats he trains in his "Skinner boxes." Viktor E. Frankl, the famous founder of logotherapy, believes that, in spite of the conditions set by heredity and environment, we are free to choose the attitude we will adopt in facing our life situations. Let's see who is right.

1. If you can control your will, you are free. (This is simply the definition of what it means to be free.)
2. If you can will to perform—or not to perform—a given act, you can control your will.
3. If you can throw "odd man out" at will, you can will to perform—or not to perform—a given act.

So—can you throw "odd man out" at will? You may have played the group game of pooling some reward, then throwing down one or two fingers at will, so that the person who throws differently from the others drops out, until only two are left to split the reward. Can you really throw down one or two fingers at will? If so, you have freedom of the will. Test it as follows:

Get a friend to command in advance how you should throw your fingers (one or two). First obey his commands. Then throw opposite to his commands. Can you switch from obedience to defiance at will? If so, you have demonstrated your freedom. I know from experience that every normal person can do so. The only exceptions are people who are severely brain-damaged or who have lost control over their muscles.

This demonstration will have shown that you have will power at your command. If you are religious, you may think of it as God Power, Divine Power, the power of God in man. If you are not religious, you might call it Personal Power. In either case it is *available* Power, the power of will, the power to make choices. With Power comes responsibility—your responsibility to use it to help yourself.

In order to use this Power within, you must release it from the "deep freeze" in which most of us find our potential Power due to disuse. We can release it only by drawing it into activity. The Power of Freedom Exercise can bring your Power into use.

The session is divided into three segments: (1) eight minutes at night before retiring, (2) sleep, (3) eight minutes in the morning upon arising. During segments (1) and (3), carry out the sequence below:

1. Repeat aloud or to yourself a *thematic priming meditation* such as the Hail Mary, the Lord's Prayer, the Sh'ma Yisrael, or the like. If you are not religious, an excellent priming meditation is the Serenity Prayer of Alcoholics Anonymous: "Give me the power to change that which can and should be changed, the serenity to endure that which must be endured, and the wisdom to know the one from the other." Even though this is called a prayer, it may also be used as simply a meditative wish.

2. For the first three minutes of the eight-minute session, build *self-confidence* by autosuggestion: repeat aloud or to yourself the following sentences:

"I am gaining self-confidence, because I am worthy of success. I will succeed. I will succeed because I cannot fail with the Power within on my side. I have the same creative Power within me that is in all people. The Power is greater than any person, but present in all people. I will hereby employ it to strengthen, guide, and sustain me." Say these sentences over and over for a full three minutes.

Now at first you will think this is a lie. At first it will be a lie, but it is a "good" lie. A good lie is one that is both harmless and helpful. If you tell good lies often enough, you will believe them yourself. And the moment you believe them yourself, they cease to be lies and become true. This is brainwashing, but it is the "good kind," that is, the kind you do yourself for your own benefit. You have a right to wash your own brain anytime you want to. You are choosing to do this exercise of your own free will, and that is quite different from having someone else brainwash you by forcing you to say aloud what they want you to believe.

3. During the remaining five minutes, think of the problem area with which you most need help now. Then let your mind relax and "fire at will"—that is, think of what it wants to. Take notes on ideas that pop into your mind, and keep a log of these ideas. Watch for meaningful patterns in them.

During this five-minute period, do your best to "let your mind go blank." You will find that all sorts of thoughts will pop up to fill the blank period. This is similar to the free association of psychoanalysis.

At first, the thoughts may be mostly negative—fears, resentment of injustice, etc. This is to be expected. *If negative thoughts become too intense, you can knock them out* by returning to *autosuggestion* and repeating several times the affirmations in it. This may be necessary over a period of some days. It is based on the psychological principle that, while you can think of more than one thing at a time, you cannot concentrate on more than one thing. So forcing yourself to concentrate on the positive knocks out the negative.

Soon you will find that the negative thoughts and feelings are subsiding and that positive material is beginning to come into your mind. Often, however, this will happen at times other than during the five-minute meditation period—at times when you least expect it, perhaps in a dream or at work.

Be sure to record all of this material in your notebook. The ideas will seem unrelated at first, but in time you will have enough elements to begin to see their connection. Then you will understand how your unconscious mind has been tapped to provide creative insights into future potential from the building blocks of past experience. From these insights will come new plans for the future, which you can use to work out present problems.

You may feel that you aren't creative, but everyone is. J. P. Guilford, one of America's leading psychologists, has done much research to show that creativity is not identical with high intelligence; and the well-known New York psychologist Rollo May has shown that the desire for creative expression is a fundamental human need, a need that everyone is capable of fulfilling if he will develop the use of the creative abilities he has.

Notice that the middle segment of the exercise is sleep, which gives the ideas stimulated in the first segment a chance to take form and find a new application to life problems; these new applications may then appear in the third segment following sleep.

You may find it effective to vary the affirmative statements in the autosuggestion step. You can alternate the previously indicated statements with the following affirmations in building self-confidence. They contain a mnemonic device to make remembering them easy. You will notice the underlined letters spell out self-confidence:

1. I am gaining in Self-confidence.
2. I will build an Excellent future.
3. My determination will Last.
4. My First step is self-acceptance.
5. Constantly I will grow in this, and Firmly I Do Exude New Confidence Every day.
6. I am using the Power within to solve problems without.
7. I do this through Freedom to choose these attitudes toward life.

If you don't like these affirmations, you can make up a set of your own. The important thing is to say them regularly.

As you practice this basic routine over a period of time, you will become aware of gaining its cumulative benefits. You will see that you can control and use at will the Power within to solve problems. You will know that you are a free person, not a rat in one of Skinner's conditioned response boxes. You will learn how to use this Power to achieve the good things of life, to "find your own bag," to "do your own thing"—in short, to gain a new meaning and purpose in life that will mark you as Somebody. And everybody wants to be Somebody.

In addition to the Power of Freedom Exercise that has just been presented, there is another exercise that I have found very effective in helping people stimulate their own creative thinking. It utilizes a well-known psychological principle that is the primary method of personality evaluation in the field of clinical psychology, the principle of what is known as a projective technique. This is why I call it The Projection of Creative Meaning Exercise.

When one interprets an ambiguous stimulus, he "projects" into it the meanings that are suggested by his unique background of personal experience. For example, an ink blot is presented, and the subject is asked to decide what it resembles. The things he sees in it give a clue to what is on his mind.

We all have deep-seated feelings and ideas in what Freud called the unconscious mind—the areas we cannot reach by ordinary means of memory because emotions block recall. When we have problems in life, they usually involve a lot of these unconscious thoughts and feelings. Often the best clues as to what we should do in the situation are hidden in these unconscious mental processes. In order to deal with the problem, we need to tap this area of unconscious mental content. There is a way to do it through various projective techniques.

These techniques bring out our intuitive thinking—ideas based on subtle subjective feelings rather than on the objective types of evidence with which pure reason deals. And intuition often suggests ways of handling a problem that we have overlooked when trying to work it out by reason alone.

We can utilize projective methods to stimulate our intuitive capacities. In the process, we will gain self-assurance and relief from anxiety and depression. These benefits follow from the fact that, as we begin to gain intuitive insights, we also experience a feeling of progress in working out our problems, and this feeling in turn helps us relax and accept our own adequacy to deal with them.

This intuitive process may or may not involve the tapping of a Higher Power—a Power beyond man himself. It depends upon whether you think there is such a Power. For those who do not, the projective technique presently to be described serves as a psychological device to aid in utilizing the power within, which we all have. For those who do, this technique can become a means of reaching the Power Beyond and allowing it to draw forth the power within, so as to find life goals and approaches to them that are in harmony with the universal purpose and design for this particular life. Most people believe there is such a Power.

What most people want is reassurance that they are not alone, that there is a Higher or Guiding Power that can be contacted in time of need. Here is a way of gaining this assurance. It is not a form of scientific "proof," and it is not intended to be. Neither the Bible nor other religious or sacred writings were ever intended as textbooks of science. They are rather based on the method of intuition, recognizing as do the existentialists the validity of nonrational knowledge.

Such knowledge comprises facts that cannot be known through experimentation but that can be sensed only intuitively. It is the basis of so-called revealed religion, and it is the heart of the relatively new fields that are scientifically known today as parapsychology and paraphysics. (*Para* because, as the Greek prefix indicates, they are outside of, around, or beyond the usual fields of science.) These fields represent what is usually referred to as psychic research, and include such phenomena as mental telepathy, clairvoyance, the influence of mind over matter, and so forth. We learned something about all of this in the last chapter.

Some scientists say there is no such thing as intuition because they can't study it by the scientific method. Many of them also say, as did J. B. Watson, the founder of behaviorism, that there is no such thing as consciousness, for the same reason. But no one really believes that *he* is not conscious—it is always the other fellow who may not be.

So if you can accept that you are conscious, you can accept that things exist that are not amenable to study by the experimental method of science. And if you can accept this, you can accept that there is such a thing as intuition. And with this acceptance, the way is cleared to use the intuitive method to advantage, to tap sources of knowledge otherwise closed to you.

Yes, there is a way of gaining reassurance through the method of intuition. The present technique helps a person gain self-assurance and self-acceptance by promoting the conviction that he can receive such insightful guidance.

It is a means of focusing and interpreting this guidance through the use of literature as a familiar background upon which the content of the unconscious (which serves as a base for intuition) can be projected. In doing so, a person can form new intuitive insights that can be the source of help with old problems—as well as the foundation of faith that there is a Power Beyond that helps with problems. We can use various kinds of literature. For the religious person, the Bible, especially Psalms and Proverbs, is ideal; for the non-religious person, Bartlett's or Hoyt's books of familiar quotations or similar material serves well.

This process is much the same as that which occurs in the Rorschach Ink Blot Test, wherein we project our own unconscious meanings into the blots. In the use of Biblical or other literature as a backdrop for projection, we call upon our past and forgotten associations to interpret the meaning of, and the connections between, various Biblical passages. And in this process we allow for the operation of this unseen Power Beyond (which is really a Power Within, according to Luke 17:21, but in order to tap it we have to look beyond ourselves to others and to reach it in relation to our fellow human beings). In the "revelation," we bring together, by an *apparently* chance process, different interpretive materials that have special significance for our situation.

The justification for the conclusion that an unseen influence or revelation occurs can be reached by analogy with the use of the Rorschach ink blots: the *apparently* random and chance-designed ten ink blots that constitute the test were selected only after Swiss psychiatrist Herman Rorschach, who invented the method, had made and discarded some ten thousand such blots. The final choices are those that suggest the widest variety of common associations to the majority of people. The apparently random and chance-determined blots were really carefully selected for meaningful content by an "unseen influence."

It can be the same in the operation of apparently chance factors whereby Biblical passages are selected and juxtaposed for interpretation of the relationship.

We could, however, believe either way on this point and still profit by the technique. If we choose to believe that the selections really are only determined by chance, we can still consider the possible meanings that are suggested by this chance connection. In this case, the procedure becomes only a game to lighten the seriousness of the burden as we attempt to think through our situation. On the other hand, if we are willing to add the unseen influence of a Higher Power, the process becomes a matter of serious search for the intention of this hidden connection.

You must choose for yourself which way to go here, and then stick to it. In making your choice, it may help to remember Alexander Pope's famous couplets as you consider which road is most satisfactory for you:

> All nature is but art unknown
> to thee;
> All chance direction, which
> thou canst not see;
> All discord, harmony not
> understood;
> All partial evil, universal
> good. . . .

"Essay on Man," Ep. I, L.289

In applying this technique of gaining new insights, we must consider some polarities: good and evil, success and failure, hope and despair, love and hate, etc. We can make intelligent choices only after such consideration, because most choices are neither black nor white, but grey. They are neither all good nor all bad, but a mixture of both good and bad. We must choose the overall best, or the overall least bad, and in order to do this we must evaluate the choices from the points of view of both their goodness and their badness.

To make our evaluation, we will pick two passages from the Bible or whatever other material we may use, and we will interpret these passages as pro and con in relation to some proposed solution to a life question. From the overall meaning that intuitively comes to us, we will make a judgment of the wisest action under the circumstances.

Now, let's get down to a step-by-step procedure in applying the Projection of Creative Meaning Exercise.

1. Write out the question for which an answer is sought.

2. With this question in mind, choose from whatever inspirational literary source you prefer (Biblical literature such as Psalms or Proverbs, other religious literature, or some secular source such as Bartlett's or Hoyt's books of familiar quotations) by pure chance a particular page. A good way to do this is to place the book behind your back and thumb through it, stopping upon impulse at a particular point, deciding beforehand whether to utilize the right-hand or left-hand page. Then look over this page with the question in mind. Does a sentence suggest something—anything—related to the question?

If it does, write down the sentence and what it suggests. If not, repeat the process until you strike a page that does suggest something.

3. Repeat this whole process twice more so that you have three sentences and their suggested relationship to the question at hand.

4. Next write down three ideas that come to your mind as you *consciously* try to reason out the answer to the question.

5. Write out the plan of action suggested by the three sentences from inspirational sources into which you have projected meaning in relation to the question at hand.

6. Write out the plan of action suggested by the three ideas based on conscious reason.

7. Decide which plan of action is most attractive to you. This becomes the *thesis,* the other the *antithesis.* Think about these alternative plans. When you are sure that one plan is best, act to implement it. If neither plan shapes up as just right, repeat the entire process above. You may wind up with the same, partially the same, or altogether different material. Make another judgment as to which plan

is best among all those that have now been considered. When you are sure that one is right (or the best that can be done), act on it.

This exercise has helped many to find answers they have not been able to find otherwise. I have received letters from former patients saying that it has been the key factor in their finding new life meaning. Of course it does not work for everybody.

And certainly it must be utilized with caution, because overdependence upon the intuitively determined answers rather than the rationally dictated conclusions may lead to disaster. It is dangerous to blindly trust this or any other projective technique in making decisions. This is why we must never jump to projective conclusions or act impulsively upon them. But when balanced by rational evaluation, they may make the difference between getting a satisfactory answer in which we can have faith and upon which we will be motivated to act, and making a halfhearted and doubtful decision that leaves us in confusion and fails to motivate effective response.

These intuitive insights occur, according to recent brain research, in the right hemisphere of the brain, whereas the left hemisphere functions in the rational and logical areas. Both sides of the brain must be utilized in determining the answers to vital questions of life. Neither side can be trusted alone.

Those who are religious will find a precedent for this exercise in a Biblical passage, Proverbs 16:33: "On the breast the lot is drawn; from Yahweh the decision comes." (The reference is to the fact that, according to the annotation in the Jerusalem Bible, the ephod worn on the high priest's breast contained the sacred lots. These lots were drawn by the priest to settle issues that could not be decided upon reason alone.) This means that what may seem to be chance, from a mechanical point of view, can be directed by a Higher Power that leaves no objective evidence of its action. The same point was made in Alexander Pope's couplets quoted earlier.

This exercise can also be very helpful to many people in deciding the basic issue of chapter 5, the first step in finding meaning—the question of whether there really is a Higher Power who guides a purposeful universe, or whether everything is merely pure chance application of mechanistic natural laws. Complete the exercise with an open mind. Do the results seem to you to be those of pure chance or of unseen direction?

In this connection two examples, one from the experience of Dr. Frankl, and the other from my own experience, may be helpful.

First, a vignette from the life of Frankl, paraphrased from his book, *Psychotherapy and Existentialism,* pp. 34-35 (see bibliography): Hitler had taken Austria, and Frankl, being Jewish, had applied for an immigration visa to the United States. Shortly before the United States entered the war he was called to the American Consulate to receive it, but at the last moment he hesitated.

The question of whether he should leave his aged parents, for whom he could not get visas, beset him. "This was the type of dilemma," he said, "which made one wish for a sign from heaven." Then he noticed a piece of marble lying on a table at home. Asking his father about it, he learned that the Nazis had burned down the largest Viennese synagogue, and that his dad had brought the piece of marble home because it contained a part of the tablets upon which the Ten Commandments are written. It showed one engraved and gilded Hebrew letter, and his father explained that this was the abbreviation for one of the Commandments, "Honor thy father and thy mother. . . ."

This event so impressed Dr. Viktor Frankl that he took it as the answer to his dilemma and stayed with his parents, allowing his American visa to lapse. He had projected into the ambiguity of these objective events an answer to a severely disturbing life problem. This answer stemmed from the use of his own creative capacities to manipulate the data of experience in arriving at a course of action, but he would not have been able to tap these creative insights without projecting them into these ambiguous events. And who can show that his interpretation of them as a "sign from heaven" was wrong?

And now a second illustration, this time from my own experience. On September 7, 1974, Hurricane Carmen stood menacingly close to the Mississippi gulf coast. A hurricane watch changed to a warning. Everyone in these parts remembered Camille in 1969 only too vividly, and we all started preparation. And for me, after surviving both Betsy in 1965 and Camille, not a small part of preparation involuntarily became anticipation.

I remembered the inevitable uncertainties and apprehensions of last-minute decisions as to what course of evasive action to take. And I reflected upon the fact that I was nearly a decade older than during the first hurricane experience and so less able to stand the strain.

I thought my residence would probably survive again as it had in Camille; but all hurricanes are, like people, unique and unpredictable, and I decided to accept the invitation of friends to weather the disaster with them. In spite of the best preparations, there is an element of insecurity, and it is always comforting to face danger with others.

As I packed to leave, I thought of the inevitable aftermath of these tantrums of nature; I dreaded the weeks of cleanup and the apprehensive inspection of the damage. I knew the danger of leaving a house: looters often arrive even before the destructive winds and water. I thought of the days without lights or refrigeration, the spoiled food, the flooded streets and houses, the broken trees, windows, and street lamps. Somehow, I thought, there must be a better way for people to live, in a safer part of the world. I wondered how much longer I could tolerate the continuous strain of day-to-day anxiety during the several months of high hurricane risk in every year.

As I wondered about all of these things, my eyes fell upon a copy of the Bible, and I thought that reading a few verses before departing would be in order. And then I thought that this was no time to tarry, for the weather reports said that by noon the rain would make many streets impassable, and it was now past eleven o'clock. I had better leave at once.

But I finally reached for the Book, promising myself that I would limit reading to only several verses, and then be gone. And I would read something easy and quick, like Psalms, Proverbs, or Ecclesiastes. And I must not take time to select a passage; I would simply slip my finger at random into the general area of these books and assume that the first chapter that caught my eye would be meaningful to me on this occasion.

By this method I opened the Bible to Psalm 57. I noticed it had eleven verses in six stanzas, and I started to look for a shorter selection, but I knew there was no time to do so. I decided to read the first lines of this psalm and somehow interpet them in a way that would have meaning for me now.

So I read the passage that I had selected by pure chance. Or was it chance? Was it a "sign" such as that for which Frankl had looked? What would you have thought, if you had been in my place and read these lines?

> Take pity on me, God, take pity on me,
>   in you my soul takes shelter;

I take shelter in the shadow of your wings
until the destroying storm is over.

What were the odds of my selecting this passage by pure chance? They are difficult to compute accurately. The part of the Bible I had intended is about one sixth of the total, and I knew roughly its location but had no clues beyond this. Even this limited area has about 300 pages; the odds of selecting any one page would be about 1 in 300. Statisticians usually consider that, if the odds of an event's occurrence are less than 1 in 100, the event did not occur by pure chance.

So was it a sign? The answer depends upon whether you believe there are such things, but to me it was a very important sign—a sign that I should take shelter in the faith that I would be protected in the storm. And this conclusion was reinforced by the outcome: after we had spent hours anxiously awaiting the hurricane's arrival, it turned in an opposite direction, and we received only moderate rain and almost no wind.

In thinking of this happening as a sign, I had projected into an objective event—the event of selecting a Biblical passage by apparent chance—the meaning that I needed in order to face my situation and deal with it. Frankl did the same with the marble chip containing the Hebrew letter.

This is the goal of projective techniques in logotherapy—to project the meanings that we need in order to face life, the meanings hidden within our own unconscious thought processes and experiences, onto the objective world of conscious awareness so that we may recognize and use them. Finding these meanings requires tapping the creative capacities we all have but usually cannot call forth at will. Projective techniques merely serve as a device to reach these capacities. You have the creativity. Projective techniques can help you use it.

When you are on the road to using your creative capacities, and when you are beginning to feel confident of your ability to apply them, it remains to set out upon the systematic exploration of the life values in which your own personal meanings may be found. But before you do, it is important to get in mind the type of goal for which you are really searching. You may be surprised by the statement that meaning in life is never found in anything—never in any*thing*. In the next chapter we will see just what are the sorts of goals in which it can be found.

Chapter 7

Encounter: The Fourth Step in Finding Life Meaning (Applied Logotherapy)

Most people believe that life meaning is found in doing something. Not so. Life meaning is found not in some*thing,* but in some*body*—in somebody for whom something is done.

Maybe you think that sounds corny, that I'm saying that you have to be good and pay the preacher and join the Scouts and all that and then everything will be all right. But this is not what I'm saying. The real message is that we get wrapped up in "things" (maybe making music, maybe making money, making love, or what not), and we get the impression that whatever we do that turns us on is our real "bag," our "thing," whereas the only reason it really gives us any satisfaction is that it (directly or indirectly, consciously or unconsciously) brings us into relationship with other beings. By their response to us, these beings—who may be subhuman (like pets), human, or superhuman (the individual's personal concept of God)—produce a feedback of acceptance and approval that makes us feel like Somebody—like a unique and worthwhile person.

Yes, real meaning in life is found not in material things, but in interpersonal relationships. Skeptical? Let's see if I can prove it to you.

The existentialist uses the term *encounter* to indicate a deeply meaningful personal relationship. It is an intimate one-to-one exchange of feelings and mutual understanding. In contrast to a rational transmission of knowledge and information, it is an emotionally toned reaching by one person for response from and acceptance by another—a phenomenon of feeling rather than of reason. The first thing to remember about emotional problems is that they always represent a breakdown of adequate relationships with other people. Thus, the prime step in becoming the person we want to be is to examine our lives in relation to others and, if we have failed to devleop that deep, subtle and intimate relationship called an encounter, to determine why. And then the task may become one of changing our approach to people with the specific aim of establishing this kind of relationship with at least one person, though preferably with several people.

Such a close relationship is not possible between any one person and a multitude of others. He who tries this winds up with his own feelings of loyalty and affection spread so thin that he fails to get close to anyone. This is often seen in the politician, entertainer, or other public figure who depends upon the acclaim of the masses. He tries to embrace everyone, but his feelings are shallow, for he cannot care deeply for people he does not know intimately, and to know anyone well consumes time. As a result, he often deceives himself into thinking that he has a huge number of intimate friends. But when adversity strikes, and he needs deep friendship, he sees it fading away as he reaches for it.

This is not to say that we cannot care for human welfare as a whole. For example, if a disaster occurs far off, we are sorry without actually feeling hurt. But if it occurs in our own neighborhood or among people with whom we have intimate relationships, we ourselves are hurt through feeling the sorrow of those we love. Such love is a possessive thing; it cannot be shared on a mass basis. So, we must choose carefully a few special contacts and develop these. Most of the time, when we develop emotional difficulties, we don't feel this relationship with anyone.

How can we go about establishing this experience? Let's look at its possible sources. We may find the satisfaction of this deep and basic need either in other living beings, or in a Higher Power (which in turn may be revealed both in relations with people and in nature). The latter we can understand only on the human level as a Being having psychological processes much like our own: loving, hating, punishing, rewarding, experiencing much the same sentiments as we, and expressing them through physical properties known to us. The feeling that constitutes this relationship to a Being greater than ourselves may be sensed in relation to a sunset, a waterfall, or a great mechanical bird in supersonic flight. Any aspect of nature or natural law may bring us this feeling of contact with forces beyond the comprehension of human reason.

Levels of Encounter

Let us look in detail at the areas that can be explored in our struggle to find meaning in the relationship between our own unique personality and each of the sources of encounter. As we have seen, there are three kinds of sources: (1) sub-human, (2) human, and (3) superhuman.

1. *The subhuman level of encounter* is that with lower animals, with pets that have been a part of a large segment of family households throughout the world and over the generations. Many people relate better to pets than to their own kind, being threatened by human relationships, in which they feel inadequate. But they always personify such animals by attributing to them human characteristics of intellect and feeling that animals do not actually show any concrete evidence of having. This shows the real need is to encounter other human beings; but when human relationships become difficult, we take refuge in less dangerous sources of encounter.

2. *The human level of encounter* is that with another person. Certainly the most concrete—and usually the deepest and most signifi-cant—encounters we experience are with other beings like ourselves, whose feelings we share and to whom we can turn for understanding and acceptance of our own feelings of awe, hope, despair, desire, and the like. In other words, we can get closest to other people. Although a Higher Power may be the central force in our experience, we are closest to this power when we are are closest to others.

As previously noted, when we have severe emotional stress, we usually experience a lack of closeness to others. It is as if no one else could possibly understand or feel what we are going through. It is as if we were standing on a barren island surrounded by an infinite, empty sea of nothingness and must cry in vain for someone to come, to comfort, to relieve, to share the terror. We are isolated and inwardly alone, and when we are thrown externally with people, our impulse is both to reach out and to recoil. We want to ask for help, but we feel that a great gulf prevents understanding. We feel we must step back lest this lack of comprehension cause a hostile reaction toward us.

We withdraw into an inner shell. Other people, whom we sorely need, and to whom we would beckon for aid, are light years away from us even though they may live under the same roof and share our daily lives. There is no feeling of desolation like that of being alone and rejected.

We may transact all sorts of business without the least interaction with people. Forced in our daily lives constantly to contact individuals in our homes, businesses, clubs, churches, schools, and neighborhoods, we may still never "encounter" a single soul.

The chances are that you have at some time had this feeling. If so, you will know it, for there is none other like it. Perhaps you have it now, though you may not want to think of it because you think there is nothing you can do about it.

There is something you can do, however. You can learn to experience a true encounter with people. You can find people who will understand, who will share your inner life, even the feelings that cannot be put into words but can be knowingly felt by two as if by one. How?

First ask yourself these questions: Which persons have most influenced my life? Which have I felt closest to? Why? What values did I obtain from them? Is this relationship still continuing? If not, is it gone forever? If so, have I replaced it with another equally satisfying relationship? If not, why not? Have I really tried? Or have I sat around feeling sorry for myself and using this loss as a justification for failure?

Why not try again now? Remember that a replacement does not have to fulfill the same relationship in order to fulfill the same needs. For example, loss of a mate does not necessarily require replacement by another; a friend or relative may have much the same value to you.

The power of personal relationships to give meaning and direction to an otherwise confused life may be seen in the story of the late Alexander King, an illustrator and a former editor of *Life*. King, long addicted to narcotics as a result of medical prescription for intractable pain, married a beautiful girl. They adored each other. After several hospitalizations had failed to cure King's addiction, his wife offered—if he could not break the habit and must spend the rest of his life as a user of narcotics—to go with him to some foreign country where drugs could be obtained legally or without difficulty. This willingness to sacrifice so much for him so moved him that by sheer will power he quit using narcotics and never returned to them.

He, like all of us, had a potential power that he had not dreamed he could muster until a purpose for calling upon it became apparent. Then he rose above his former limits without knowing how. All he needed was a reason. A reason in this sense, however, was not just a logical reason—which he had always had, for logic told him that addiction was disastrous—but rather an emotional reason based on a deep sense of a worthwhile purpose in life. When he perceived that someone else could so love him as to suffer for him, he sensed a mission in preventing the necessity of that suffering. This kind of love showed him he was Somebody, and knowing that brings out the best in us all.

A patient of mine was a girl who had been in a lot of trouble with men, both married and single. Her mother did not think she could change, but she suddenly gave up her socially disapproved behavior and did not return to it. Sensing that nothing had occurred in therapy to account for this much change, I asked the source of her new motivation. "Only through a special boy friend's belief in me was I able to do it," she replied. "My mother didn't have any faith in me, and neither did anyone else except my boy friend. But he trusted me and knew I could do it, and I could not let him down." Just another case of hidden potential that was waiting to be called forth by purpose. And again the purpose was emotional and not rational. The girl had known rationally all along that she needed to change, but both she and I knew that she would not until she had a better reason.

This personal encounter is also the basis of religious conversion. We may, in fact, consider the experience of Paul as the Great Encounter. In every type of conversion, this same kind of meeting takes place between the mind of the convert and that aspect of life that has become meaningful to him. While it seems that some people are able to find this kind of deep meaning in various aspects of nature—in the outdoor life, in the beauty and majesty of the natural world, or in the marvelous discoveries of science—the vast majority of us experience an encounter only with another human being. It is not necessary that the personality involved be known to us in the flesh. Paul, for example, had probably never met Jesus of Nazareth, whose existential personality he encountered on the Damascus road. We may encounter any of the great personalities of history when we come to feel the same sense of mission that motivated them, although there is undoubtedly a special added quality in the intimate in-person contact.

An encounter is involved in experiencing love, religion, and family life. The factors involved in these aspects of life cut across all of the other aspects, for they represent values in both creativity and experience and may also involve values in attitudes. But it is not necessary to have a family in order to live a meaningful life, nor is formalized religion essential to meaning. For example, family values may be obtained by a maiden lady in teaching others' children, and religion may be expressed simply as reverence for life. The central value of both family life and religion is love, which is needed by everyone, and which occurs in every true encounter.

How can you go about establishing an encounter? Decide upon several human beings to whom you feel closest, and arrange to exchange thoughts with them on the subject of what is worthwhile in life. Share your deepest feelings. You will find a lift and inspiration that can come from no other type of experience. If you are shy, making yourself do this will be hard but it will be worth the effort. You will see together some things that none of you have seen individually.

A logical place to begin is with friends and relatives. Of course, it is possible that you are in strange surroundings with no people of your own. But if there are human beings in your environment, it is probable that at least some are potential friends.

You can't just walk up and say, "Be my friend, for I need you." But you can walk up and say (in effect), "Be my friend, for you need me." Preposterous? Not if you use your natural ingenuity to spot opportunities.

Here is the story of how one individual took advantage of this principle. Alone on a new job in a large city, he needed desperately to make some friends in what Wordsworth described as "the crowded solitude" of anonymous metropolitan living. He knew that strangers could be dangerous, but he also knew that most of those working in the same office building would have at least something in common with him. If he could meet them, he could pick out the ones with whom he had mutual interests. So he contrived the means to get acquainted. To step in and introduce himself would immediately create suspicion that he had an ulterior motive or was too naive to be interesting. Instead, he arranged to get people to introduce themselves to him.

He watched for chances to offer a service that they needed. A favorite gimmick was to look for times when likely prospects were fumbling for a match. He didn't smoke himself, but he had match folders printed with his name, address, telephone number, and business. He would leave a folder with each person who needed a light. Later, when they saw him in the building, they generally stopped him to ask about the matches. It seems that the heads were colored red, white and blue, and each match burned with a flame of the same color as its head!

Another of his gimmicks was to ask for the time. When it was given, he set his watch while the prospective friend stared. The timepiece contained an alarm mechanism, which startled onlookers as he managed to set it off in adjusting the hands. His pockets were loaded with conversation pieces, although he never played a practical joke. He wanted to make friends, not enemies. These devices seem unsophisticated, but they work.

A lonely woman with no job and the same need to meet people rejected the idea that her only hope was to get picked up in bars by questionable characters. Instead, she volunteered her services as a hospital grey lady. There she helped attend a dying cancer patient whose grateful husband gave her a job in his office. A year later, this husband became her own.

The principle is always to make another need you; he will then be willing to fulfill your need for him.

Did you say you have no chance to meet people? There are opportunities awaiting you everywhere. Here are just a few of the more obvious:

1. Join the YMCA or YWCA. The activities will offer both exercise and companionship; and if you are worried and lonely, you need both.

2. Enroll in a dancing class. This too provides an opportunity both to exercise and to socialize. If the class is offered by a commercially operated school, be sure you read the contract carefully before signing.

3. Seek out groups of special interest. There are clubs for almost every sport from archery to water skiing and for nearly every hobby from ceramics to rocketry, as well as more serious literary, philosophical and political societies.

4. Attend a Sunday School class. Regardless of your faith, you can find a congenial group if you visit a number in rotation until the right

one leads you to settle there. And even if you are an atheist, you can find in some of the liberal churches people whose thinking will stimulate and challenge you.

5.   Enroll in adult education classes. Most cities have an extension school from college or universtiy, if no institution of higher learning has a campus there. And the majority of even relatively small towns have either some work of this kind or adult night classes under sponsorship of the high school.

6.   Volunteer your services for USO activities, grey lady hospital duty, or social work. All such organizations need help as badly as you need to meet people.

7.   Take a battery of aptitude and interest tests from a counseling and guidance psychologist. You may discover unsuspected abilities and long-stifled interests that are waiting to be developed and that may open up new avenues to human contacts as well as new goals in life.

8.   Investigate (with caution!) an introduction bureau if one is available in your locality. But do not get snared by the lonely hearts correspondence clubs; most of the members are not what they seem. Sometimes, for example, a man assumes a woman's name and sends a fake picture in order to induce other men to send gifts of money or jewelry. More often the correspondent is simply a very poor risk, especially as a matrimonial prospect, because of a long history of emotional instability.

On the other hand, some of the metropolitan introduction bureaus are operated with reasonable care, and when you can go for a personal introduction before committing yourself to social activities with the prospect, this service can fulfill a real need. The better bureaus try to find out at least a little about the background, traits, and qualifications of all applicants, even sometimes superficial personality tests. This helps somewhat to place genuinely suited people together, but you can find out more about this suitability in a half-hour face-to-face meeting than by any screening methods available to such services.

9.   Attend AA meetings. For the problem drinker, there is a group of special advantage in most communities. While Alcoholics Anonymous turns some problem drinkers off, this lay organization helps more people than any other single method of treatment. And even if it is not for you, it offers an excellent source of contact with other persons who share the common goal of a desire to lick the alcoholic problem.

The stranger you need most to encounter may be a very familiar stranger—may, in fact, have been your husband or wife for years, but one you may never have really met. If so, isn't it time to get existentially acquainted, to experience this encounter?

Before I came to the Gulf Coast, a woman whose husband I knew in the Rotary Club called in great distress. She was beautiful and charming with a devoted spouse and lovely children. Those who knew her assumed that hers was an ideal family, and yet she was now desperately asking for help in saving the marriage. While clinical treatment was available, if necessary, it became obvious from the conversation where the trouble lay. This couple had drifted so far apart in playing their separate family roles that they no longer dared communicate their difficulties in fulfilling these roles. Each tried to cover his problems and struggled to believe that all was well. But each knew deep within that both were experiencing trouble.

She was advised to make a time for a genuine encounter with her husband in order to unburden her true feelings and to draw out his bottled-up emotions. The two had lain together in deep affection for years without being able to communicate their love. Each was afraid that his or her inadequacies were letting the other down.

Nothing was heard from her for some time; then she called to happily express her gratitude for the advice. It has opened up a closeness the two had not experienced since the first years of their marriage. Their troubles, while real, were now working out because they were being shared. Each had learned to offer understanding and to receive it in return, and this prevented the eventual necessity for expensive clinical treatment that otherwise would have been the only alternative if the marriage was to be saved.

Remember this principle: Don't ask but offer; make yourself needed, and you will fulfill your own needs, because the real basis of our need for others is our need to be needed by others. This is one of the deepest urges in human nature. Through being needed, we gain status, love, response, and fulfillment of the psychological requirements mentioned earlier. It is the satisfaction of these that in the last analysis gives true meaning and purpose to our lives; that gives us a cause to live for, a feeling of being a genuine person with a job to do, a role to play, a mission to carry out—that convinces us that we are Somebody. And the person who feels like Somebody has everything.

It may happen that the routine or past associations represented by family and friends are inadequate for the closeness you need because of the particular nature of your past experiences. It could be, for example, that the particular way of life that you have made your own through education, travel, or other experience is quite different from that of your early training. In this case, you may have to look to new contacts. As an example, you may have become disillusioned with the beliefs of your family religion after learning some things in school that seemed to conflict with these beliefs. So you quit going to church and no longer feel close to the people there. But you have not found any new contacts to fill the void; you have been drifting instead, with a sort of empty space in this area of your life, never becoming consciously aware of this fact. If you learn more about both science and religion, you will find that there is no conflict. You may, however, decide that the old church no longer fulfills your religious needs; in this case, you may seek values in a new religious group.

This situation occurs frequently among college students. When I was a college professor, I had many occasions to counsel young people with this problem. The solution is to see that the values of a true religious experience are not bound to any one set of theological beliefs, and then to search for the form of religious expression best suited to your particular emotional needs. This inevitably involves building the relationship of a true encounter between yourself and religiously inclined people who hold the same values.

It may be that the main obstacle to a deep and genuine encounter with the people already in your life is a set of firmly ingrained habits that have become so automatic that you tell yourself you cannot break them. For example, perhaps you are so used to irritating people by a lack of tact that you justify yourself with the thought, "That's just the way I am and I can't help it." Then it is time to ask yourself a basic existential question: Have I really assumed responsibility for the course of my own life?

Have you genuinely believed in your own freedom to choose what you will make of it (within the limitations of heredity and environment)? Or have you let yourself off the hook by telling yourself that these factors in your life have left you no freedom to choose, that there is nothing you can do to solve your own problems and to straighten out your difficulties with people, and that all you can do is feel sorry for yourself?

If this is the case—and it usually is—the next step is to admit it and turn back to tackling the wall of resistance within. Turn once again to the relationships you want and need in your life, and take a long, second look. Search yourself honestly, expecting that you will unconsciously try to justify your efforts as all you could have done.

Ask yourself these questions: Have I blocked myself in my attempts to get close to the important people in my life? Have I fallen into the trap of long-established habits of escaping my own responsibility by telling myself I have been unjustly dealt with, unfairly treated, and that the failure isn't my fault? Think all of this through carefully. Is there some telltale evidence that you have not done all you could, that you have not assumed full responsibility for all of the choices that are open to you? For example, if you are tactless, have you tried your best to learn tact? Have you studied the way tactful people handle situations that give you trouble? Or have you deceived yourself into thinking that it is not necessary for you to change because it is the duty of others to accept you as you are? If you sense such marks of self-deception, start once again to struggle with the problem, and this time watch yourself every step of the way, repeating these questions to yourself at frequent intervals.

Now, if you have carefully examined yourself and concluded that you are not guilty of self-deception, that you have taken full responsibility for all you could do, and that failure results from factors beyond your capacity to remedy, stop. Accept the fact that the chances are nine out of ten that you are still rationalizing, still defending yourself, still being blinded by your own feelings of resentment of what life has done to you. Accept this and look once again at the encounters in which you have failed, at the problems that you have considered unsolvable. Again ask the existential question: Have I taken full responsibility for trying everything I possibly could, have I tested my ingenuity to the limit of its capacity?

If, after repeated trials, you have come to the point where you can say only that you have truly done your best within the area of all choices open to you, the next step is in order: turn beyond yourself for help, thus looking both within and without for assistance. The emphasis should still be on the view within yourself, for in the last analysis outside aid can only guide you in turning back to your own resources and seeing the true potentialities within. But you may now be in need of this outside help, and it can be instrumental in changing your life.

The wisest move for most people at this stage is to turn to a minister, priest, or rabbi. If you have no religious leader, it may be a good time to get one, although this is not to say that you cannot conquer emotional conflicts without religious affiliation. There are other sources of help, but there are few better for most people, provided you choose the right religious counselor.

This does not necessarily mean that you have to be religious. Sincere religious leaders are interested in people, not in proselyting. They will try to help you as a person, not as a parishioner. A poor pastor who has no training in or understanding of emotional makeup may do real damage. But most present-day clergymen, at least those whose churches require a high level of education in their leaders, are familiar with and practiced in the handling of emotional stress, and they can offer comfort, understanding, and guidance to a troubled mind, regardless of one's religious belief or lack of it.

If you do not already know a minister who has the reputation of helping people in distress, ask around for one. And if you already have a minister, but he is not the understanding type, look for another. When you find him, tell him your feelings honestly and completely. Admit the real need you have for people, your feelings of rejection, isolation, and despair, and your need for help in finding your way.

It may seem at first that there is no point in seeing a minister if you do not already believe in a Higher Power, but this does not necessarily follow. The pastor's ability to create an encounter with you may well supply the needed stimulation of your innate ability to encounter others in your life, even though he may not be able to meet you on any common religious ground. So do not hesitate to talk to the right minister even if you are an atheist; he will understand your feelings and encourage you to express them, and you both will gain an insight into them. The close interchange of sentiment between the two of you may be just what you have been needing to get started in working on your other relationships. You may well be led to find faith or to increase the faith you already have in a Superior Being; or you may leave still an unbeliever. The right religious leader will offer you as much of himself in the second case as in the first, and you may have been enabled to find yourself. Perhaps later you will find the Higher Power.

One of my women patients, while recovering from a severe depression, resented the fact that her religious faith had apparently let her down at a time of crisis; she found herself unable to pray as she customarily had. She knew she needed the understanding and encouragement of a spiritual leader, but, unfortunately, her rigid, old-fashioned pastor drove her further into a protective shell with his pious platitudes that showed no understanding of human nature. She withdrew into another period of guilt-laden depression, and it was only after a difficult period of treatment that she was again ready to search for the answers to her spiritual questions.

This time she was directed to a pastoral counselor with clinical training, and he knew how to draw out and deal with her religious feelings. In a short time, she had resolved her conflict and was again able to make prayer the important part of her life that it had once been. Through an encounter with this understanding man, she regained her ability to establish an encounter with a Higher Power. Her relations with her husband and her daughter improved, and once again she knew that she was Somebody.

Visit different religious services and listen to the pastor. If he seems the sort of person in whom you could confide, try him. If not, try another. You will find the right one. The important thing is to locate one with whom you can feel comfortable, who seems to understand, who reaches out and touches you with a confidence that immediately relieves your tensions and dispels your fears—and to whom you feel the urge to reach out in return. In other words, one with whom you can experience a true encounter.

In your struggle it may happen—and usually does—that you become very aware of feeling physically ill. When you are worried, anxious, or depressed, you always notice more readily the little aches and pains that we all have, and they may become big and terrible pains that incapacitate you for routine daily work. Some of them may be imaginary, having no real basis in bodily processes other than those of the brain itself; but most are quite real, brought on by disturbed functioning of the various organic processes that are affected by emotion. When you worry, you emote; there is an underlying element of fear. When you resent something, you emote; the basic process is one of anger. And all emotion is accompanied by well-known physiological processes that, when they become too intense, can interfere with normal functions and can literally consume and destroy the body.

Witness the case of the well-known stomach ulcer. Certainly the pain is not imaginary; the process involved can result in a very real hole in the stomach. Fundamentally what happens is that, when you worry, the processes of digestion are interfered with; worry is a form of fear, and fear always stops or slows down digestion. Fear triggers bodily processes designed to protect you in dangerous situations, and in danger a quick source of energy is needed. So, instead of trying to obtain this through hopelessly slow digestive processes, the body calls on the liver—which is a sort of silo for stored energy in the form of blood sugar—to give up a part of its reserves. Digestion is forgotten, although there may still be food in the stomach. Digestive juices become imbalanced, and powerful acids are oversecreted.

When you worry, you usually don't feel like eating, and your diet and meal schedule become disrupted. Digestion starts to work, then becomes blocked by emotion, then works a little, and so on. Pretty soon, strong digestive acids are in the stomach without proper food intake, so the acids, having nothing better to digest, start eating into the stomach lining. And before you know it, you have an ulcer. The consequent pain has a definite physical basis, but it is of psychological origin, having begun with anxiety.

Some physiological effects of emotion usually accompany the emotional and psychological disturbances of a breakdown in your relationships with people and the subsequent struggle to find a basis for the encounter you need. You may have all sorts of medical symptoms that in reality are psychologically caused. These can run a very wide gamut, but the most common are given here.

1. Stomach and intestinal disturbances (indigestion, stomach cramps, diarrhea, constipation, nausea, loss of appetite, gas, and the like).
2. Headaches (migraine, bands of pressure and tension on the scalp), ringing ears, and dizziness.
3. Back pains, especially in the small of the back.
4. Excessive sweating, especially in the palms and under the arms.
5. Irregular and rapid pulse and the sensation that your heart is skipping a beat.
6. Excessively heavy breathing, possibly with dizziness or blackouts.
7. Excessive fatigue, feelings of boredom and listlessness.

The above are merely the most common; any other symptom that you experience as physical ill-being should be considered. Do you have any of these signs of anxiety? If you do, the first thing to remember is that any one or all of these, as well as a large number of other symptoms—in fact, a good proportion of all known medical complaints—can be caused either by physical or medical factors (such as a germ, a virus, or hormone imbalance) or by psychological and emotional factors. You cannot tell the difference by the way you feel; only a physician can determine whether the causes of your particular symptoms are physical or psychological.

So, when you are worried and begin to pick up any sensations of bodily ill, it is essential to see your physician. He will be able to treat the medical aspects and to reassure you about the nonmedical factors, and if you are fortunate enough to find one of the relatively few doctors who still take time for discussion of your emotional life, you may find in him the source of encounter that has been the object of your needs.

Even if he is the impersonal type, he can tell you whether your emotional symptoms have progressed to the point of requiring specialized handling by a psychotherapist, or whether you are likely to be able to deal with them adequately yourself. He may give you tranquilizers or some other medication to relieve your tensions and to tide you over while you are working through the problem. At any rate, if you feel physically disturbed in any way, you won't know where you stand until you have seen your doctor. And if the disturbances occur from the first of your problem, you should see him before or together with the minister. You can put together what each tells you into a total plan for action that will bring rest to both mind and body, and peace to the spirit.

There are other sources of help: perhaps a favorite teacher (if you are not too far removed from school days), or a senior business associate, or anyone who befriended or counseled you in the past. The key here is to find someone to whom you can unburden yourself when you have become so entangled in human conflicts that you can no longer think clearly alone. Establishing such a relationship will bring out in the open your confused feelings about your problems, and you will see them in a new light. But the most important thing is that you will have found someone with whom to share and exchange feelings, and you will know that you now belong to the human race, that you are on the way to becoming Somebody.

I had to learn the hard way to encounter people, for I had been so busy all my life studying them that I had had no time to know them. If an art student held a magnifying glass to a Van Gogh painting in order to study the brush strokes, it would be difficult for him to see the overall effect of the finished work. In the same way, a student of the elements of behavior can miss the human being found only in the total picture. This is what happens to most psychologists and psychiatrists unless they get to know people outside of the professional situation.

In my case, I began to feel a true encounter with people only when I began to develop the method of spiritual encounter (to be explained later). In connection with this, I learned, as previously stated, that the way we make a relationship to a Higher Power become most meaningful is through developing relationships with people. When I began to find others who were looking for this same thing, and to search for it with them, I began to feel that I belonged to a cause and had a meaningful place in life among those who also belonged to it. Then I started to look for ways in which I could serve this cause, and it came clear that one of my best ways was through helping my patients to find their own worthwhile causes. As I experimented with methods of doing this and began to find techniques of successfully guiding them—the ways that are described in this book—I came to feel the reward of becoming Somebody in helping others find their own avenues to the same goal.

The superhuman level of encounter is that with a Higher Power. In the last analysis, the deepest form of meaning life assumes for you is determined by your attitude toward a Higher Power. You may believe either that the universe is the product of design or that it results from chaos, but you have to come to grips with what you believe before you are able to make meaning of your own life in relation to life as a whole. Whatever your conclusion, it is an important one, for it conditions how you will proceed in facing life's problems.

If your belief is that purpose or design is lacking in the universe, you can still, like the French philosopher Sartre, build into your own existence a purpose in terms of what you value in this chaos as worth living for—and if need be, dying for. In this case you must, as it were, keep up your own morale and lift yourself by your own bootstraps, for there is no help beyond man himself. The existential principle of freedom to make—and therefore responsibility for—your own choices as to how you will face life still holds, but you can expect to encounter only other people like yourself in your experience.

On the other hand, if it seems reasonable to you that there is more to the universe than can be understood in terms of chance—if, indeed, it has become clear to you that natural laws are merely man's generalizations of observed happenings in nature, and that no one can show any obligation on Nature's part always to behave in this way, although she for some unknown reason does (at least in man's limited experience); if you can sense in the worlds of the telescope and microscope a glimpse of things felt but unseen; if you can grant on faith that there is in the scheme of things some sort of purpose and some kind of Being superior to man himself—then you have open to you another, and in reality far greater, source of existential encounter. (As noted earlier, we get closest to a Higher Power through encounter with people, but this presupposes belief in the Power.)

This third source of encounter is called *spiritual encounter*. The best way to determine if it is for you is to ask yourself whether you have ever experienced what William James, the founder of American psychology, who wrote the first important book on the psychology of religion *(Varieties of Religious Experience)*, called a sense of presence. This is an awareness of an unseen Being, as if someone were behind you in a room and you could sense the person by clues too subtle to pinpoint but still sufficient to convince you of the presence. It is not necessarily related to institutional religion. Some preachers never have the experience, while some who never go to church do.

For those to whom it is suited, I have outlined a step-by-step plan for spiritual encounter in my book *Everything to Gain* (see Bibliography). I have used a modification of this plan myself for fifteen years now, and it has been one of the most valuable aids in my life. It requires only a few minutes in the evening and again in the morning. I have missed only one-half of one day in all of these years, and I have done the exercise only because I experienced personal benefit. If your make-up is anything like mine, you also will benefit from it.

The Act As If— Exercise

The attainment of encounter relationships can be facilitated by a special exercise designed to build self-confidence in dealing with people. It is an extension of the Power of Freedom Exercise, the first part of which is also aimed at building self-confidence. However, the Power of Freedom Exercise is limited to thinking, and in the present exercise, we go beyond thinking to action.

The Act As If— Exercise, as I call it, enables us to translate imagination into activity and thus to obtain visible evidence of action's effectiveness in improving our relationships with others. In this exercise we develop the habit of *acting as if*— acting as if we were the successful, self-confident, capable personality we would like to become. It goes a step beyond Norman Vincent Peale's "power of positive thinking" to the *power of positive action*. We first think positively by imagining what kind of person we would like to be. Then we act positively by doing at least one thing such a person would do. The more we act this way, the more we feel the part; and the more we feel it, the easier it is to act it. Soon it becomes ingrained in us, and we are no longer acting. The general idea of this procedure was suggested to me by an old book, *The Philosophy of As If*, by H. Vaihinger (New York: Harcourt-Brace, 1924). I developed the idea as an exercise and had been using it with patients for several years before I discovered a similar concept in *Wake Up and Live* by Dorothea Brande (New York: Simon & Schuster, 1936). More recently the value of this approach has been pointed out by Maxwell Maltz in *Psychocybernetics* (Englewood Cliffs, N.J.: Prentice-Hall, 1960). But none of these writers employed the principle in a formal exercise to be practiced in a specific manner, and this is required in order to make it work most effectively in building the habits of self-confidence and self-acceptance.

A word of caution here: this is not to condone acting as if you were something you should not or could not be. An untalented person cannot become an artist by acting as if he were one. This is where many of the pseudosophisticated go wrong. You cannot gain respect by acting as if you had done something worthy of it when you have not. This would simply be narcissism, which would defeat the very goal you wish to gain. The correct approach is to act as if you were the personality you want to be and should be—not as if you had already gained the achievements that you might wish or may in the future attain. Act as if you were Somebody, not because of great achievements, but because you are you.

Act as if and you will be surprised to find that you will soon come to believe it true. And it then will become true. The only reason the opposite has been true up to now is that you have believed in that and acted as if it were so. It is just as easy to move over to the other side, the desirable side. Try it and you will become convinced. But you must be prepared for an initial period of discouragement during which you won't yet believe in yourself and will have to depend strictly on the process of acting as if you believe.

You cannot change your feelings at will. What you can control through will power is behavior. Thus, the place to start is with the power of positive action. Act as if you were what you wish to become. You can make yourself do this even though you may not believe in it at first. Accept it initially on faith, and after a short time you will see the results. Then you will automatically begin to think positively. And the Bible tells us, "As he thinketh in his heart, so is he." You will then become what you wish to be. The results all depend on your getting started, and here is where you need the philosophy of "as if." You will be amazed at the results.

The Act as If— Exercise can be most effectively applied by following the steps outlined below. Each step requires only five minutes a day, any time during the day that you choose. Only one step is ever done on any one day.

Step 1. Solo setting

We begin in a completely nonthreatening circumstance, one in which it is almost impossible to fail. For this step choose a situation where for the next five minutes you will not be in contact with any other person. If someone should unexpectedly show up, abort the procedure and start again later in the day when no one is around. (And similarly in each succeeding step, if the unexpected occurs, abort the step and start again later.)

During this first step, for which a good setting is usually a walk alone, you are to think, feel and *act* for five minutes *as if* you were the secure, self-confident person you would like to be, the person who would succeed at whatever he tried, even though you may not yet have decided upon anything to try. How would such a person walk? How would he carry himself? Would he swing his arms, or whistle? Would he look down at the ground, or hold his head high? For this five minutes, act as you think such a person would act.

The chances are that you will carry this first step off without a hitch the first time, and that you will be ready for the next step the next day. But if for any reason you do not feel secure or comfortable in it, repeat this step again the next day, and until you do feel secure.

Step 2.   Stranger setting

Now choose for the five-minute period of practice a place where you will come in contact with some person, but a person unknown to you. A good setting for this exercise is also a walk, this time in a location where there are strangers, such as a park.

In this step, arrange to pass a stranger, and during this period, *act as if* you were the secure, self-confident person you would like to be, the person who would succeed at whatever he tried. How would such a person react as he passed a stranger? Would he speak in this particular setting? If you think he would, do so; if you think he would not, don't. Be this person during that five minutes.

Now the chances are good that you will have no trouble with this second step; but if you do, repeat it the next day, and until you are comfortable in it. It is possible that you might decide to speak, and that you might then be rejected by the stranger; and that might shake you up. If something like this happens, repeat the step as indicated.

Of course, if you should be rejected and this doesn't bother you, you have already accomplished the goal of Step 2, and you are ready to go on without repetition. But in this case, be sure you are not rationalizing when you tell yourself the rejection does not bother you—be sure you really feel this way. If you don't, you will defeat yourself by going ahead prematurely.

Step 3.   Acquaintance setting

In this step, choose for the five-minute practice period a location where you will be brought into contact with someone you know casually. A walk may be a good setting for this step, too, if you can arrange to pass someone whom you would consider a casual acquaintance.

Repeat the usual attitudes during the test period. How would the self-confident, secure person you would like to be act in this situation? Would he stop and chat, or would he nod and pass on? That is the way you are to handle it.

If this step results in anxiety or any other difficulty, repeat it on subsequent days till you have mastered it.

Step 4.   Personal friend setting

The location for this five-minute practice period may have to be changed, unless you can conveniently contrive to meet a personal friend while taking a walk. If you can, walking continues to be an excellent setting.

If your friend is one with whom you are comfortable, you may feel very secure. But you do risk something, since you are now acting as if you were the self-confident personality you would like to be, and this may not be the way your friend is used to thinking of you.

The object of this step is to confront those who know you with a new image and to get them to accept it. This may take a number of days, during which you consistently play this new role. If so, it is wise to repeat the exercise on some days with the same friend and on other days with another friend.

As you progress, you will find that any surprise your friends may show will probably form a pleasant surprise for you. The reason for this is that, when you assume a more positive attitude toward yourself, you will inspire an unconscious response on their part of a like nature. And in turn, this will inspire you with still more self-confidence, which you will then reflect in your *acting as if*— and gradually you will cease to be acting at all; your feelings of self-confidence will become genuine and fully true.

Step 5. Conflict setting

The final step in your practice is to place yourself for a five-minute period in contact with someone who constitutes something of a threat to you—someone with whom you have had some degree of friction or conflict. Here again you act as if you were fully self-confident and secure in your ability to handle this interaction in a satisfactory manner. You do whatever you think a secure, self-confident person would do.

When you can successfully handle this step, you have it made: you will have learned to believe in yourself as you interact with others, and you can use this self-confidence in building encounter relationships.

This last step may require a number of days of repetition before you master it; on the other hand, you may make it on the first try. But if you do feel successful and comfortable with the step almost at once, you should repeat it at least a second time to be sure the feeling is genuine. And the chances are that you will later meet more frustrating circumstances that will lower your self-assurance, in which case you will need to review and perhaps repeat the entire series of steps.

This Act As If— Exercise can be of great and continuing value to you in maintaining the self-confidence necessary to continue successful everyday relationships and to accomplish the aim of this chapter, the establishment of encounters with other beings. Do not forget that these encounters are the real core of meaning and purpose in life.

In the next chapter, we will take up the matter of finding specific tasks that give life meaning through the status they create in the eyes of others who are possible sources of encounter.

Chapter 8

Dereflection:
The Fifth and Final
Step in Finding Life
Meaning
(Applied Logotherapy)

Dereflection is the core of the logotherapeutic process of searching for meaning and purpose in life. This term is used by Frankl to denote the action of drawing the individual's attention away from his failures, inadequacies, shortcomings, misfortunes, and liabilities, and focusing it instead on his good points, successes, aptitudes, and assets. Only in this way can he find new goals and aims that will make his life purposeful and worthwhile. Only thus can he discover tasks that will bring him into sufficient relationship with the "significant others" in his life (as psychologist O. H. Mowrer has called them) to make his existence meaningful.

In the last analysis this is a spiritual (though not necessarily religious) process, because, as Frankl emphasizes, real meaning in life is never found in material things or within ourselves alone, but always through extending ourselves beyond our own boundaries of material desires to the needs of others. And this is the essence of spirituality.

Once you have come to grips with the necessity of establishing interpersonal relationships and having an "encounter" with at least a few other beings (as indicated in the last chapter), you are ready to explore all your life experience for something to do that will stimulate and perpetuate these relationships.

But what if you have not yet found the right sources of encounter? Must one in this situation wait until he has found them before searching for a life task? No, not at all. The truth is that many people find the task before they find someone for whom to do it.

And in a few cases, that someone is never real, but only imagined. In others, the someone hasn't even been born yet, and the individual does his "thing" for future generations who will understand and appreciate it.

An illustration of this last point occurred one summer when I was on the staff of Dr. J. B. Rhine, the famous parapsychologist, at the Duke University laboratory. While on a research grant to study his techniques, I was at lunch one day with his chief assistant at that time, Dr. Gaither Pratt.

"Why," I asked Gaither, "do you and Dr. Rhine choose this hard way of life when you could take so much easier a road? You could simply be college professors and teach away and enjoy weekends with no flak from your colleagues, no unpleasant criticisms from the scientific community; but instead you choose to fight this battle of ESP and psi phenomena against a steel wall of oppostion from the 'orthodox' scientists, you elect to be sneered at, to be put down by your colleagues as crackpots and pseudoscientific charlatans, and to devote your total life energies to this unpopular cause. Why?" (Of course I knew at least part of the answer, because I knew my own reasons for identifying myself with their battle, but I wanted to see how Dr. Pratt would respond.)

"We are aware that we may not get any credit for this work in our lifetime," Pratt answered, "but we know that a time will come when it will be proven even to the most adamant skeptics that we were right. And that will be our reward."

Now both Rhine and Pratt get along quite well socially. In fact, Rhine is an especially magnetic personality, which accounts for his ability to raise the money over the years to pay the laboratory expenses, since the university paid only a small portion of these. Neither of them was having any difficulty in establishing the encounter relationships needed in life, but both were turning for additional relationships to people of the future, who might not even have been born at that time. Their meaning in life was to a considerable extent being furnished by the contemplation of the feedback that would be given by these dwellers in a time yet to come.

This is often true of scientists, writers, and artists. Many highly creative people who do not receive full acceptance by their contemporaries turn in fantasy to the future.

But what about the hermit on the mountaintop, who says he hates all people and has a machine gun mounted and ready to spray anyone who dares come up the mountainside? How, you may ask, does he fit the claim that everyone needs somebody else, that life meaning is found only through extending oneself beyond himself to others?

If you look more closely at people of this type, you will find that they have pets that they personify, or perhaps a "spiritual encounter" (which may include memories of those formerly dear to them, and whom they do not fully accept as dead or lost), or they may show evidence of looking to the future for as yet undetermined contacts. In their fantasy lives, they want and need somebody, even though on the conscious level they sincerely believe they want nothing to do with anyone. There really are no exceptions to the rule that life meaning is found only in other beings, and not in things.

Before going further in the process of searching for meaning, it will help you to sharpen up awareness of what values you hold. Keeping in mind just which values are strong and which are weak in one's individual life experience will enable the determination of whether a prospective life task will be meaningful to him.

To that end complete the following scale, and then study your high and low values. Keep them before you as you consider each possibility for a meaningful life activity. Does it contain at least some of your high values and avoid at least most of your low values? Unless you can say yes to these questions, you will do well to look elsewhere.

The Meaning in Life Evaluation (MILE) Scale

Directions: The following list of twenty values is summarized from answers given by a large sample of individuals who were asked which values they most want in life. You can easily determine which are most important and which are insignificant to you by the following rating technique. It should be noted that you *cannot* make an accurate evaluation merely by *ranking* the values in order of importance in your life, because often we get tangled up in what we have been taught about how we ought to regard them and thus fail to see how we really do feel about them. But the rating technique to be described will avoid to a considerable degree this problem by making you think much more deeply about each value, not just in terms of its particular meaning to you, but especially in terms of its meaning in relation to all other values. The final result will be a more accurate appraisal of the things that you want most and least out of life, and on the basis of this knowledge you can evaluate how well potential activities fit your needs.

Opposite each of the twenty values you are to tabulate (in the same fashion that you record scores in dominoes, one line for each point) the number of times you would choose this value in comparison with each of the other values. For example, starting with "wealth," you first compare it with "lasting friendships." If you would prefer wealth to lasting friendships, you tabulate one point for wealth. If you would prefer lasting friendships, you tabulate one point for lasting friendships. Next you compare wealth with "physical sex," the third value on the list. If you would prefer wealth, you tabulate another point opposite wealth; if you would prefer physical sex, you record a point opposite physical sex. Then compare wealth with "a good name" in the same fashion, and so on until you have covered all twenty values. The result now will be a score for wealth ranging from a minimum of zero to a maximum of nineteen.

Next you take "lasting friendships" and compare this value with all other values.* Every time you choose lasting friendships rather than another value, you record a point for lasting friendships. Every time you choose another value you tally a point for that value. Again the score can range from zero to nineteen. Then you repeat the process, taking next physical sex and comparing it with each value below it in the list; and so on with the entire list. Your final comparison is no. 19 with no. 20.

Your highest-rated values will be those to emphasize in any life activity; the lowest-rated values will be those to avoid.

You may think that, if you had some of the values, you would automatically have many others. For example, you might feel wealth would bring a number of the others. But rate each value as if it were independent of all others. You might feel that wealth would afford you

---

*Starting with physical sex, the next value *down* the list. Notice that you do *not* return to wealth at the top of the list, for you have already made that comparison.

physical sex, but in comparing the two, assume they are independent. If you could have only one, which would you choose?

Now here are the twenty values to rate:

1. Wealth_____
2. Lasting friendships_____
3. Physical sex_____
4. A good name (high character)_____
5. To be remembered favorably after death_____
6. To gain romantic love_____
7. To be a great leader of people_____
8. Health_____
9. To be a hero or heroine_____
10. To be of great service to people_____
11. To be famous_____
12. To be physically powerful (males) or beautiful (females)_____
13. To be an intellectual genius_____
14. To find adventure and new experience_____
15. To be happy_____
16. To understand the mystery of life_____
17. To fulfill religious goals and obligations_____
18. To have peace of mind_____
19. To gain social acceptance and belonging_____
20. To gain a personal identity_____

After you have rated each value and tabulated the results, there is an important consideration in using them. You might find that you have among your high values no. 15, To be happy, and no. 18, Peace of mind. And you may feel that if you had these, all important others would automatically be included.

Actually it is just the reverse: if you have the things that offer a real meaning in life, happiness and peace of mind will follow as by-products. Logotherapy teaches that happiness and similar goals can never be successfully sought as ends in themselves; they occur only when we cease to concentrate on them and work instead toward a worthwhile purpose that fills our lives with a sense of personal significance and identity. It is only when we transcend ourselves by going beyond our own selfish interests, only when we extend ourselves to the world of others around us, when we lose ourselves in pursuit of goals that make us valuable to others, that we really sense our own self-value and personal worth in a way that produces the warm glow of happiness and peace of mind.

So if you have fallen into the trap of placing too high a priority on happiness and other values of personal satisfaction as goals to be sought in themselves, now is the time to rethink your way through the real meaning of your life and to zero in on those values that can truly work in the quest for happiness—those values that are in and of themselves aimed, not at your own happiness, but rather at the happiness of others who are significant in your life.

Life Values

We have learned that in logotherapy there are three basic types of life values: Creative, experiential, and attitudinal. You will remember that the significance of these terms is as follows:

Values are the meanings in life that are experienced by a group or culture as a whole. For instance, patriotism has traditionally been a value in most societies. A meaning is an individually desired goal; a value is an objective sought by the group as a unit. A particular person might not accept patriotism as a personal meaning, although it might be generally regarded as very important by the group.

Logotherapy teaches that we must each find our own personal meanings in life—the goals that can give our individual existence a sense of direction and worth, and through which we can receive a feeling of identity as Somebody. In order to do this, we must explore all of the values of our own as well as of other cultures, so that from them we may glean the ones we can incorporate into our own personal life. This is not to say that we can take off on our own with no respect for cultural or social approval, but rather that we must choose the forms of culture and society that are in harmony with our individual life meanings, and that we must find within them expression of these personal meanings.

Creative values result from some type of creative activity. Such values may range from the procreation of children to the collection of garbage. Not only the fine arts (such as music, painting, and litera- ture), but also the most mundane of everyday activities may serve as a creative outlet for some people.

Experiential values are gained by experiencing the creative work of others, as well as by communing with nature, and all activities that represent a human experience that brings enjoyment or a sense of significance in life.

Attitudinal values are those values that still remain when we experience a hopeless situation we cannot change creatively or experientially. This involves our human freedom to choose how we will meet an unalterable fate, such as a terminal illness. The attitude we take toward the conditions that we are forced to face will determine whether we incorporate them into our experience as a significant part of the purpose of our life, or whether we fall beneath their weight in a fit of hopeless despair. If we have succeeded in finding an unconditional value in all human life, through the perception of man's uniqueness in relation to the universe, we are in a position to fend off despair in the wake of an apparently meaningless fate by choosing the attitude that this fate is itself an integral part of our unique personal worth.

As we noted in Chapter 4, Saul of Tarsus journeyed along the dreary road to Damascus with a lot of time to think about the real meaning and purpose of life. And the more he thought, the more the sense of a great and important mission that he had seen in these little groups appealed to him as his own. Here, at last, was something for which he had been searching throughout a drifting and undirected existence; here was a place to put his life, something to fight for, to suffer for, to live for, and if need be, to die for—something to make his life worthwhile. All of this suddenly came to him like a great flash of light, and from that moment on he was a new man, Paul the Apostle, a man with a purpose—a purpose that justified his life and, when the time came, his death.

But today, you may object, there is little to match Paul's type of experience; there are few missions that can appeal as did the cause of early Christianity or the great revolutionary causes of the past. Some young people found such a cause in the radical movements that appeared on college campuses. But many young people now have revolted against the excesses of the past and are trying to work within the political system rather than trying to foment a revolution.

Some people turn to crime in an attempt to make meaning of a hopeless world. The ultimate in this direction is illustrated by a recent newspaper story of two teen-aged soldiers who went AWOL in response to army pressures. Together they murdered seven persons. When caught, they insisted that they had done the victims a favor by taking them "out of this stinking rat race." One of the men had on one arm a tattoo that said, "I hate the world." They both wanted to die together, welcoming the death penalty because "man suffers when he comes into the world and suffers when he goes out."

These boys considered their lives (before as well as after their crimes) untenable and hopeless. They did not see that their acceptance of this fact was what had made it so, and that their resultant uncontrolled hostility toward the world had forced them into hopeless defeat. But they did experience an intimate and understanding relationship with each other, two lost souls in search of a common unattainable meaning: they had an encounter. In each other they found their only meaning, the only intelligible aspect of an otherwise hopeless world that did not understand or care about them; and together they found a purpose in proclaiming the futility of life. In defying life and facing death together, they found meaning in suffering the outrages of a meaningless universe. In this suffering, they were unconsciously pointing up and protesting what they thought should not be, and they were making everyone aware of it. Unfortunately, their methods of protest were purely destructive and in the long run could result only in their own destruction.

It is important to find a genuinely satisfying cause before you are tempted out of frustration to grasp at illusory short cuts. And such a purpose, to be most fulfilling, must carry the great courage that can be born only of deep conviction.

An example of a mission that embodies these true values is seen in Alcoholics Anonymous. This laymen's group, bound together by having faced a common problem and shared a common understanding and feeling, has developed the most successful method of treatment to date for chronic alcoholism, although many cases respond neither to this nor to any other known therapy. The essential features of AA are the encounter between the alcoholic and others who can share, understand, and encourage his fight; and the attainment, if he is successful, of a mission to fulfill in helping others face and conquer the same problem he has overcome. The plan is basically spiritual, in the sense of the word we have learned, although not necessarily religious: the participant is required to call upon "a power greater than himself," whether he as an individual believes in a particular concept of God or holds to an abstract generalization of some sort of universal intelligence. The cause of the successful participant in AA is to carry the message to others, thus fulfilling his own need to be needed. This becomes a meaning in life that gives him the courage to go on when the road again becomes rough, the strength to resist the temptation of returning to alcoholic escape when the pressures of daily living again mount. Everyone needs the psychological values that are found in AA.

If you are willing to sweat out some of the search techniques to be covered presently, you have an excellent chance of gaining a new view of life, of finding a creative cause that will offer the same values as AA, a way to share your search with others, and, through the encounter of this sharing, a mutual goal. It is important to bear in mind that, for most of us, the deepest meanings are always found in relation to other people. This is another way of saying that love—which is the fundamental form of genuine communication between human beings, and which is needed by everyone—is the primary source of meaning and mission for most. So the best way to start looking is *with* someone else, though you may have to look also *for* someone with whom to look. This is the message of the previous chapter and the purpose of the continuing exercise on encounter.

Some Special Activities That Can Help You Find Creative Values

To gain a start in the search, try the following suggestions—one each day—for analyzing the values and goals that lie deeply hidden within your own personality. Write out in detail each of the exercises. They can help you to discover your own unique creative abilities.

Exercise 1. Personal identity through history

If you could be any person in history you wanted to be, whom would you choose? Why? What value does this person represent? What do you now have—if anything—in your own life that represents this value? Make a list of ten such persons, starting with your first preference, then going to your second choice, and so forth. For each choice, write the answers to each of the questions, then look over the values involved. What does this list of values tell you about yourself? Where does it suggest that you want to go in life? Keep the results in mind.

Exercise 2.   Picture identification as expression
of values

Leaf through some pictorial magazines and select a picture that especially appeals to you. Write out the answers to these questions: Why does it appeal? What value is represented by the appeal? What do you now have—if anything—in your own life that represents this value? Do this ten times with ten different pictures, and look over the values involved. What do they tell you about yourself, about what you want out of life? Keep these results in mind.

Exercise 3.   Personal misfortunes as indications
of potential meanings

Write out a list of the misfortunes that have occurred to you over your lifetime so far, the occurrences that—regardless of how they were caused—have given you the most trouble and produced the most suffering and regret. This list may be long or short, depending upon your individual life experiences. For each item on the list, write out the answers to these questions: In what way has this misfortune handicapped you? To what extent have you—or can you—overcome the handicap? What possible advantage could it have created for you that would not have existed otherwise? What value of importance to you could such an advantage be utilized to fulfill in the future? How can you go about doing this?

At first you may react negatively to this exercise, wondering how there could be any advantage to your misfortunes. But there is an old saying that out of every evil some good always comes, if you look for it. Even destructive hurricanes afford an opportunity for new building and fresh starts that otherwise would not have occurred. Look for what is there for you.

A good example of how this can work is shown by the series of actual events dramatized in the well-known movie *The Stratton Story*. Monty Stratton, a Chicago White Sox pitcher who lost a leg in a hunting accident, turned the tragedy that at first appeared to end his career into a personal advantage: he became the first person ever to play professional baseball with an artificial leg.

This is not, of course, to say that we should *seek* misfortune in order to find a way of accomplishing something we otherwise could not have done. Logotherapy teaches that there is no value in self-inflicted suffering, but only in unavoidable suffering. The latter comes to most people sooner or later, however; and when it does, we can find a purpose and meaning in it. This occurs through realizing some positive value that accompanies the misfortune, but which is easily overlooked unless we search for it.

Exercise 4. Personal uniqueness as a source of meaning

(1) Write down the year you were born. Why were you born that particular year instead of any other in five thousand years of recorded history? Was it pure chance? Or was there a purpose behind your living at this time? Write your opinions. (2) Where were you born? Was the place determined by pure chance? Or could there have been some plan to this? Write out your thoughts on these questions. (3) Into what family circumstances were you born? Rich or poor? Good family relationships or bad? A life of comfort and happiness, or of tragedy and sorrow? As part of some minority group of religion, race, politics, or other division? Or as part of a majority group in any of these divisions? Does it seem reasonable that all of this occurred by pure chance? Write the answers to these questions.

Then ask yourself whether you can really believe that all of these things occurred by pure chance, or whether there is meaning and purpose behind them. Is your personal uniqueness—which results from the complex combination of all factors of your individual makeup, and which marks you as different from all others who have ever lived—only a chance result, or are you somebody special, with a special job to do in life as a result?

As you think upon these things, it is likely that your personal life will begin to take on a new appearance of meaning and value. You will probably see some values in it that you had not noticed before and sense some ways in which you can use this uniqueness that is you alone to advantage in realizing these values.

Exercise 5. Symbols as expressions of values

Choose any word that pops into your mind and express its meaning to *you* by a symbolic drawing of some sort. For example, you might express the idea of patriotism by a flag, or the concept of peace by the well-known peace sign or by a dove or by anything that suggests peace to you. The Chinese language has several combinations of characters for peace. One combination is the sign for mouth plus that for rice: rice in the mouth means peace. Another combination is the character for woman plus that for roof: The woman in the home means peace. What means peace to you?

And what symbol means to you whatever word you choose? Record the symbol. Then ask yourself, what value lies behind this symbol? Repeat the whole process ten times, and then take a look at the ten symbols. Do they suggest any common value, or perhaps two or three values? The values they represent may well be among those of greatest importance to you.

These are simply a few exercises that can help you to explore your own life experience for the *creative* meanings which are potentially rich for you.

Values in Experience

These values, we have said, are those that come from knowing the world about us, from enjoying the sensations it affords, and from putting these things together into a more meaningful picture of the world. In presenting the ways of realizing creative values, we have just considered some special activities that involve everyday life experiences. There the aim was to help you find the real motivational center of your personality, in order that you might see more clearly the type of task that could give the greatest direction to your life. Here we are concerned with experiences for their own sake, although they will add to your awareness of the other types of values. Here are some suggested activities for making the most of your experience (try a different one each week).

Participating in an overview of the world of art

Attending an opera, a symphony, a play, or an art gallery offers experiences that may be added to those of the world of science, to be mentioned presently. The two areas complement each other, for art is man's expression of his reaction to the life given him by the natural world. And here we come to the real crux of the matter of finding meaning and purpose in life, for art expresses the wishes and fears, fulfillments and frustrations, anxieties and despondencies, and hopes and encouragements of other human beings who have faced this same search. It shows the significance they have attached to these experiences, and finding such meanings for ourselves is stimulated by examining those held by others.

The visual arts are a major source of inspiration. Examining modern abstract art is a good technique for discovering the values that are most fulfilling for you, regardless of whether you like this type of art. Either in a gallery or from a book, select a number of abstract paintings or sculptures. Look at them one at a time with as completely blank a mind as you can muster, and let the association suggested by each work of art run uninhibited through consciousness. (This is not unlike the famous Rorschach Ink Blot Test used by clinical psychologists.) An advantage of having the art works at home either in books or as separate reproductions is that you can add to their effectiveness by using both sight and sound at once—through recorded background music of various types. Gradually you will learn the best combination of music and visual art for you, and you will make associations which, when studied later from your notes, will tell you the things in life to which you attach the most significance, the things you value and need most, the things that have the deepest meaning for you.

And in this connection, another form of art—literature—can be most helpful. Along with all the experiences so far mentioned, reading about how others have searched for their own meaning, what they have found and where, will stimulate your own thinking. Here such works as Somerset Maugham's *The Razor's Edge*, Stewart H. Holbrook's *The Age of the Moguls, The Rubaiyat of Omar Khayyam*, Kahlil Gibran's *The Prophet*, Edward R. Murrow's *What I Believe*, Viktor Frankl's *Man's Search for Meaning*, Ernest Hemingway's *The Snows of Kilimanjaro*, and, of course, the Bible, offer a wide variety of approaches to life which should give you some ideas. Along these lines, select several pieces and record their meanings for you.

Participating in an overview of the world of science

Looking through a microscope or a telescope and visiting a museum or a zoo will yield a wide background for sensing a unity in the natural world to which you can relate. Take part in as many such activities as you can, and record your impressions.

Attending a variety of religious services

The objective here is to gain an understanding of the orientations from which people of differing cultural backgrounds approach the meaning of man. The services should include Catholic, Protestant, and Jewish methods of worship, as well as those of other faiths if available—regardless of your own religious preference. It does not matter whether you consider yourself religious. This activity is to expose you to the cultural meanings represented by various faiths. In them you may sense a personal meaning quite apart from the organized religion represented. Record your impressions.

Visiting a metropolitan area

Visiting for a period in the heart of a great city, such as New York, San Francisco, Chicago, or New Orleans (unless you already live in or are very familiar with a large city) will afford a picture of a lot of contemporary American life, and you may see some things that have never before meant anything to you. Spend a day or more in a city. Take a sightseeing trip if one is available; if not, learn the points of interest and arrange to see them. Incidentally, this may also be an excellent opportunity to visit a museum, library, planetarium, or concert hall in order to get the material for the earlier exercises.

Taking a primitive camping trip

Camping out in a forest (unless you are already very familiar with this way of life) can be especially meaningful immediately following and contrasting with a visit to a great city. One of the best ways to sense a unity and meaning in the whole of life is through successive contrasting experiences. Consider how these apparently contradictory events fit into a bigger picture. Take a camping trip at least overnight (with someone who knows this way of life, if you don't) and record your impressions.

Travel

Visiting many different types of locales, from the mountains to the sea, as well as new and different parts of the country—and foreign lands if possible—will furnish a breadth of understanding that can be gained in no other way. Take a vacation tour if you can. If you are unable to go in person, you can gain much of this experience vicariously through travelogues, pictures, and travel books. Whichever you do, record your impressions.

Values in Attitudes

When we have achieved our best and have experienced the finest of which we are capable, the attitude we take toward the end result can give a deeper meaning to it all, even if we have not succeeded in everything we tried. The following are some important points in achieving values in attitudes:

The search for happiness

Notice that we have not spoken of any values in relation to happiness, for happiness is not the goal of the present search. This may surprise and perhaps disappoint you, but if happiness is your chief goal, you are not likely to find it through reading this book. Or any book. Or in any conscious and deliberate effort. For happiness, as Frankl has pointed out, is not something that can be gained as you would acquire a job or a wife; it is rather a by-product that comes of successful striving toward goals that give ultimate meaning, purpose, and direction to your life. It is produced by movement toward significant ends rather than by achieving ends in themselves.

It has been said that happiness is like a butterfly: if you chase it, it flitters away; but if you ignore it, it is likely to settle upon your shoulder. Suren Kierkegaard, the great Danish theologian of a century ago who unwittingly developed the existentialist movement, said that the door to happiness opens to the outside. That is, happiness is inside a little room, and the harder you push inward as you try to enter its door, the tighter you close the door. Happiness can be found, but it cannot be sought; it can be had, but it cannot be bought. So, if you would acquire it, your best bet is to forget it, and to think instead of how you can make your life worthwhile through fulfilling values that will make you Somebody.

Happiness is the enjoyment of the hunt rather than the conquest of the hunted. And this is the objective of the methods we have described, methods that can aid you in the search for your own system of values. Happiness consists in becoming, not in being. Therefore, as long as you are striving, as long as you are on the road to becoming that which you wish to be, you are moving toward the only happiness that can be achieved.

The meaning of suffering

If travel in this direction seems to fail, you need not despair. To be successful, you must be prepared to face failure; to find the good in life, you must be able to accept the bad. This means that you must be ready to suffer, to endure what you cannot change. Frankl considers suffering a value of attitude that makes one aware of what should not be, of what is not right; it points up what ought to be, and what is possible. And, as we have seen earlier, this "ability to contemplate the possible" is the chief capacity that, according to the philosopher Max Scheler, distinguishes man from the lower animals. Frankl says that only while in the state of tension created by suffering can we understand the difference between what is and what ought to be.

The role of suffering in life is to force us to face the inevitable and unchangeable forces that sometimes close in upon us, thereby limiting the area within which we remain free to choose but never reducing this area to zero, and therefore never taking away our freedom and responsibility for choice. The attitude we take toward suffering determines how we will use this freedom and what we will make of this responsibility.

Failure always produces suffering, and suffering always involves some kind of failure. Failure may result from conditions over which we have no control. Lack of success does not imply lack of meaning; it may, in fact, yield an attitude toward the resultant suffering that is more meaningful than the desired success would have been. For example, as Frankl notes, seldom would one honestly want to strike out of his life his unhappy love affairs, for these have generally matured him and may have given him more than did the successful love affairs. Pleasure alone is incapable of giving meaning to life, for it can be made real and significant only by awareness of the complementary experience, suffering. The understanding of this feature of hardship can make it bearable. Frankl loves to quote Nietzsche's statement, "He who has a *why* to live can endure almost any *how!*"

"This is all well and good," you may say. "But when catastrophe strikes, it isn't so simple to suffer meaningfully as to theorize about it." True, but in any event, all of us have to suffer; and when the chips are down, we have the choice either of doing it without hope and purpose or of grasping a meaning that we did not see before. This is in reality not unlike the praying we do in an emergency. T. DeWitt Talmage, a great preacher of a past generation, said, "Few men pray more than several times in their lives, though they may say their prayers nightly. We really pray only when, having reached the end of our human means, we must go farther."

The heights to which we can rise when the last avenue of escape is sealed are truly amazing; under such circumstances, our best is often drawn from a potential we never dreamed we had. This opportunity often comes unexpectedly, as it did to the passengers of the *Titanic*.

The greatest steamship of its day, the *Titanic* was believed to be virtually unsinkable; but on its maiden voyage, after collision with an iceberg, it sank. There were only a few lifeboats, and on April 15, 1912, on its floundering deck 1,635 men, women, and children, singing a Welsh hymn, met death with a dignity and courage they would never have believed possible an hour earlier.

Most of us are not required to face this type of situation. We ordinarily deal with less dramatic problems, but our task of finding the kind of purpose that can give new courage is equally real. And the longer the future that lies ahead, the more important is this job, for without it the road meanders aimlessly.

In one of my logotherapy group sessions, we were discussing the problem of how to find meaning in misfortune. By coincidence, a psychological intern was visiting the group to observe this type of therapy. Dr. James A. Walker, then a doctoral candidate in counseling psychology and now a practicing psychologist, illustrated the point at hand with a true story from his own life, which he has given me permission to reproduce here.

> When I was nine, a supposed friend of my father killed him with a knife. My mother, then pregnant, was left with five children, of whom I was the eldest. During the difficult years that followed, in which we all suffered great hardship because of this loss, I often felt an intense hatred for the murderer. In time I managed to handle both the family responsibilities and my education, but while away at college I still often wondered how I would react if I should come face to face with this man who had cost us so much. I knew I would one day have to face him if I were ever to be free of him.
>
> Later, during a visit to my home town, I was in a café, and this man entered and sat down at the counter beside me. Since I was by then in my twenties, he did not recognize me, though I immediately knew him.

Though I had never known just what I would do, I turned and spoke to him.

"I don't believe I know you," he said.

"I am James Walker, and you killed my father when I was nine years old."

This giant of a man began to tremble. I said, "I have forgiven you."

He extended a quivering, rough, hamlike hand, and his voice broke as he replied, "This means more to me than all of the preachers I have ever heard. I found no peace during the years I spent in prison, and I've had none since. I'd give anything in the world if I could go back and change all of that."

This encounter meant everything to me; at last I was free of the hatred. During later years, whenever I have returned to my home town, I have gone by to see the man, and this has freed us both. But I could do so only when I began to see the tragic loss of my father as part of the total meaning of my life. By hating I could destroy only myself, and it would not turn back the clock. But by adopting an attitude that this suffering was meant to be a part of my life and that I could use the experience as a source of growth of character and understanding of the problems of others, I was able to accept life as it had occurred and to find in my circumstances a job to do that made it all worthwhile.

This is what we always have to do in the case of unavoidable suffering. If we will explore the possible meanings of the experience, we can find some way in which we are stronger as a result of having had it. And from this strength, we can gain a new identity that we could not have had if the misfortune had not occurred.

The finding of faith

Einstein said, "The ultimate understanding of human existence cannot be achieved by reason alone, but only by belief." This agrees with a fundamental doctrine of existentialism: in the last analysis, meaning is made final by faith, which is belief cemented by feeling.

How can you gain such faith? It comes to different people in different ways, but the most convincing method for many is the sharing of a view by others. This is what the social scientist calls *consensual validation*. If everyone else perceives an object as you do, you are convinced that it is there; but if others should not see it, you would become quite confused as to what you are really experiencing.

The present period might well be called the Age of Uncertainty, for there are so many conflicting values and philosophies that many people find it hard to believe in anything today. There is, however, always encouragement and hope in mutual sharing among those of like kind. If you will seek out others who hold your own values, and if you will unite with them in a common bond to further these values, your faith in these values will be sharpened and reinforced.

This, in turn, leads to the desire to share with others what you have found yourself, for the deepest meaning comes from a need to be needed, a need to be useful and, therefore, recognized and accepted as important. The more meaningful we can make our understanding of others, the more this understanding means to us. This is the way we become Somebody.

Analyzing Your Discoveries

When you have systematically tried out all of these techniques over a reasonable period of time, you will then be ready for an appraisal of what you have found in life that is truly meaningful and worth centering your future upon. Go back over the exercises in search of a pattern. What central theme has kept cropping up as the focus of your desires? What particular feeling has been aroused repeatedly? What great task looms as needing doing?

If you have examined yourself carefully, you will have caught yourself with frequent thoughts of how wonderful it would be if only you could accomplish such-and-such, and you will have noticed that these thoughts flitted in and out of conscious awareness, each time being dismissed as unrealistic. Here is where you should now center your attention. This doesn't mean that you are going to realize all your wildest dreams, but rather that working toward the most practical goal related to them is likely to yield a greater sense of usefulness and personal worth than you have believed possible.

You may have to struggle harder than ever, but the fight will now mean something. It will be worthwhile. You won't mind the sacrifice, because you will have something that is worth the cost. You have previously been telling yourself that you could not achieve what you wanted most in life, so why think about it? The difference now will be that (and this is hard to believe *before* you try it) the systematic experiencing of the activities you have just been through will have given you a subtle new understanding of just how you *can* do some things that you have never previously thought attainable. And this will bring new courage and fresh motivation to put out your ultimate in effort.

Suddenly you will seem alive again; you will have a mission, a purpose that makes your personal existence meaningful. You will no longer be drifting halfheartedly through life without any real task to complete; you will now be a determined person who is experiencing the identity that lies deep within your unique individual personality.

Now you should be coming close to the point of finding a real sense of meaning and purpose in life, a direction for the future that will give you an identity as Somebody with a job to do that makes your life worthwhile. You should have a pretty good idea now of any hang-ups that may have been keeping you from finding and consistently maintaining a life meaning, and you should have made progress in eliminating them.

The sum total of exploring all of the three areas of life values for your own meanings will be a record of your own unique *character*. It will help you to understand yourself through awareness of what matters to you in life, and in turn to work out means of achieving these things. You should study these features of your own character in terms of the following factors, which are considered to be its essential components.

According to the National Character Laboratories of El Paso, Texas, directed by Col. Alex J. Stuart, Jr., there are seven such components of moral character:

1. Moral stability (the desire to do what is right).
2. Ego strength (the ability to nonconform).
3. Superego strength (the desire to adhere to a moral code). Freud introduced the term *superego* to mean what we usually call conscience.
4. Purpose in life (Frankl's spirituality, a belief in an intrinsic meaning and purpose in all human life). Of course the overall goal of logotherapy is to find one's own purpose in life; but the way he will proceed is determined, as we have earlier seen, by his attitudes toward the nature of the world and of man. So one component of character is represented by these attitudes.
5. Spontaneity (ability to express emotions comfortably).
6. Friendliness (the ability to relate comfortably to others).
7. Absence of strong feelings of hostility and guilt.

Consider yourself from each of these seven angles. How do you measure up to the desirable end of these traits? If the answer is, Not very well, you need to note carefully your particular deficiencies and to see what you can do about them. You will not find a genuine meaning in life that will challenge you and carry you over the rough spots when the chips are down until you have a basic foundation of character upon which to build this meaning.

If you lack it now, you can't make the corrections overnight. Some deficiencies may require professional help. For example, if you are riddled with feelings of guilt and hostility, you probably can't change this alone and would be wise to seek psychiatric assistance. Books on self-help can be of some value in such situations, but it will be easier and safer to go to the professionals. In some cases, it will be vital to do so, and you can't determine this yourself. The best rule is, when in doubt, seek professional aid.

To the extent that self-improvement methods can do the trick, you may find the special technique to be described in the next chapter essential. And if professional services are needed, logotherapeutic techniques will not conflict with them, since logotherapy is not psychotherapy.

Logotherapy works on the conscious level of free will and personal responsibility for actions, and on the principles of rational thought and reasoning. Psychotherapy works on the level of unconscious repressions, and on emotional catharsis or ventilation of feelings to uncover and defuse these repressions. It probes down into the depths of the mind, while logotherapy reaches up to the heights of the mind. So they both can take place at the same time, though you should, of course, be guided by your professional therapist as to these activities in combination.

We will now assume that you have either satisfied yourself that your foundation of character will enable you to proceed, or that you are in the process of getting any help you need on that score. In either case, let us look together in the next chapter at a special logotherapeutic technique and see how it can enhance your search for the right activities to add deep meaning and purpose to your life.

Chapter 9

Logoanalysis: A Special Technique of Applied Logotherapy

The present book is self-contained in the sense that you can apply logotherapy through it without other material. But if you are sold up to this point and really want to go deeply into the exploration of all human values to find what is there for you, my earlier book on my own special techniques of exploration, which I call *logoanalysis,* may be the best next step. The book is *Everything to Gain: A Guide to Self-Fulfillment through Logoanalysis* (Nelson-Hall, 1973. See bibliography.)

I chose the term *logoanalysis* for two reasons: First, to indicate that the person who is using the method is not necessarily "sick." The word *therapy* is from a Greek word meaning "treatment"; and treatment is thought of as being for sick people. So the word *logotherapy* might sound to many people like treatment only for the mentally ill.

This is not true; Frankl emphasizes that the state of existential vacuum that logotherapy is designed to treat is a human condition and not a mental illness (although it can combine with symptoms of mental illness to produce what he calls a *noögenic neurosis,* as we learned in chapter 4). He has evidence that more than half the general population suffers from some degree of this existential vacuum, or a lack of real meaning and purpose in life. Thus logotherapy actually works most frequently with people who are not mentally ill, but who lack a real goal for which to live. But because so many people misunderstand this point, I prefer to avoid the concept of therapy and to emphasize that we are analyzing our life situation in order to find a new *logos*, "meaning," in it.

The second reason I use the term logoanalysis is to distinguish my particular method of doing logotherapy—through a series of rather formalized exercises—from other logotherapeutic techniques. The essential core exercises are scattered through the present book. You can analyze your life for new meaning on the basis of these exercises alone. But if you really want to go as deeply as possible and to utilize all of your available resources in the search for meaning, my book *Everything to Gain* is devoted entirely to the description of exercises aimed at this end.

Combining the exercises therein with these in the present volume will yield a more complete picture in your search for meaning. I would therefore recommend it especially for those who may have progressed through chapter 8 of the present book with some remaining doubts as to what they really want to do with their lives.

If you feel secure at this point in your search, if you are convinced that you have now found what you are looking for in life, if you now feel the powerful motivation toward this goal that can carry you over life's rough spots and can keep you from copping out through alcohol or other means of escape when the temptation to run from these problems grows strong—if you are in this fortunate situation, you need nothing further except to commit yourself to this goal and to act upon the commitment. But if you are not so fortunate, you can profit from the other book.

Each logotherapist has his own ways of applying the basic principles of logotherapy. Frankl said, upon the occasion of the establishment of the Institute for Logotherapy at the United States International University in San Diego: I have defined logotherapy, but you who practice it will create it. I have offered the generic principles, but you will develop the specifics. (This is paraphrased from his exact words, but the meaning is unaltered.)

Most of us working in the field of logotherapy have published books on our own methods (see bibliography). My particular methods are largely technique oriented; that is, they seek to offer you something concrete in procedure in a step-by-step fashion, as you progress along the journey of searching for life meaning.

Some others approach the search in a play-it-by-ear fashion, utilizing on the spur of the moment whatever content is suggested by the direction that conversation on the subject happens to take. This may be best for some individuals; but I have tried both, and I have found that most people respond better to the challenge of a specific procedure. They need something tangible to work with.

I think one major reason why psychoanalysis, which today has lost much of its former popularity, was in vogue for so long is that it is highly technique oriented: it offers a definitely structured procedure in which the psychoanalyst has been highly trained, and it moves according to very specific rules within this procedure. Although its duration is indefinite (that is, it is a long, drawn-out affair with no definite ending point—other than when you run out of fifty dollars or more an hour), it does move along the lines of expected results that can be analyzed in terms of steps.

Psychoanalysis is a "dynamic" therapy. That is, it probes into the deep unconscious processes that motivate the behavior behind one's "symptoms." These in turn are always expressions of the ways in which one runs from, or defends himself against facing, his emotional conflicts. In contrast to this, logotherapy, like all forms of existential therapy, is a "cognitive" or rational approach to problems on the conscious level. Logoanalysis goes a step further to pin down the conscious procedure in concrete steps. Logotherapy does not conflict with psychotherapy (including psychoanalysis), and in fact a person may pursue both at the same time. And the combination is often very fruitful. Now whether you follow only the present book's techniques or add to them those in *Everything to Gain,* you will be doing logoanalysis. Both books involve this step procedure; but the earlier work contains a far more elaborate set of step-by-step exercises, and in combination with the present volume offers a far greater variety of exploratory material. And the more you explore, the more likely you are to find what you are seeking.

It is entirely up to you to choose what to do at this point: whether to work through the exercises in *Everything to Gain,* or to settle for what you now have done with the present book. If you choose the former, it will take you at least a few weeks and may require a few months; but if you need to do this, it will be worth it. You will then be ready to take on the commitment in chapter 10.

If you choose to stay with the present book, we will assume you are already prepared for this commitment.

Chapter 10

Commitment:
Dedication to
Achieving Your Goals

If you were to look up in the dictionary the word *commitment*, you would find that, in everyday use, it means something like a contract or an agreement. But the existentialist and the logotherapist use this term in a somewhat special sense. While a contract or an agreement could also be involved, the concept here is more than either of those. It has a deeper meaning, connoting a real dedication to the achievement of some goal, a burning inner desire that motivates the individual to do his utmost to accomplish something in which he firmly believes. And the goal is always something that gives him a sense of personal identity, of being Somebody, through doing something that is evaluated as worthwhile by someone else.

If you have at this point really found something in life that is meaningful to you, a task to perform, something to do with your time—whether for pleasure, profit, or principle—that gives you a sense of purpose, you will also feel the deep need to accomplish it that is called commitment.

Bear in mind that, while it may seem that you are committed to the task for its own sake, the truth is that—as we learned in chapter 7 on encounter—the real commitment is always to some*body,* and not to some*thing.* We talk about "doing our own thing," but the thing is meaningful only because it makes us Somebody to somebody. So if you have now found something worthwhile to do and someone for whom to do it, you are ready for the final dedication to this goal.

The "thing" may fall into one or more of three categories: (1) a vocational activity that you follow as a livelihood; (2) an avocation or hobby, which may cost rather than make money; (3) a cause to fight for, to work toward, to believe in strongly enough to sacrifice whatever you have to in order to fulfill it.

The "someone" may be a being at any of three levels: (1) sub-human (a pet), (2) human, (3) superhuman (a spiritual being, which most would call God). All of this we have, of course, already seen in chapter 7.

It remains only to review these meanings and to determine whether you have now found them. If you're sure you have, you're in great shape. But what if you have not? Where do you go from here?

The answer is, Back. That is, back over the chapters to see which steps you have yet to work out in finding meaning. If you skipped the application of logoanalysis in chapter 9, which requires working through my book, *Everything to Gain,* it may now be wise to go back and pick up that procedure.

If you have already done this and still haven't found the meaning in life to which you could offer a real commitment, you will need to backtrack over the present volume and look again at each step. You will see which of the steps you have not satisfactorily completed. Start again on these steps. Such repetition is always easier, and you will make it the second time around.

The odds are good that this won't be necessary if you have carefully done your "homework" as you have proceeded through the book. In this case, you will be aware of the goals that are worthy of the energies of your commitment, and you will be eager to get started toward them. The chances are that you will have already made some progress in this direction.

At this point, it may help to offer some illustrations of what it is like to have this commitment. You will see it in people you know and in those you recognize through public media and literature.

These examples represent a greater degree of commitment than that ever achieved by most people, and you may not find a cause that will create in you such burning devotion. But they can show you what an ultimate goal is like, in order that you may approach it as nearly as possible.

I am going to give two opposite types of examples, one from a religious orientation and the other from an antireligious point of view.

Because religious zeal has been a main motivator of mankind throughout history, it is easy to find examples in this area. And because logotherapy fits so well with religion (although, as we have noted, Frankl emphasizes that it is per se a secular system and in no way dependent upon religion), many people tend to identify the two. Since this happens, I want to include an illustration of the fact that it is possible for some to find the same deep commitment to goals of burning personal meaning in antireligious fields.

And in this connection, it should be noted that the depth of commitment to a life meaning in no way determines the ethics of the meaning. In other words, you may have equal devotion to a goal that is socially constructive or one that is socially destructive. Hitler certainly demonstrated that he had meaning in his life and commitment to his goals. From a logotherapeutic standpoint, he achieved success, but from a humane standpoint he was one of history's most colossal failures.

You have to determine the moral and ethical significance of a goal from the standpoint of your own personal value system. In the case of goals like Hitler's, you have to ask yourself, Was Hitler the kind of person I would like to be? Would I like to wind up as he did? Would I like to be remembered as he is? If so, it is not only your right, but also your responsibility to make this choice for yourself. But you also have to be prepared to take the consequences of whatever choice you make.

With all of this in mind, let's look at the two opposing examples of commitment.

The first is from religious literature, the story of Paul the Apostle. We have already sketched his life story in chapter 4, and there is no need to repeat the details here; but you should at this point turn back to that chapter and reread the story of his dedication to the meaning and purpose that he found in the early Christian movement.

Here is a very clear instance of a man who at first lacked any real meaning in life, even though he was well born and comfortable and had all the material things most people seek. Without knowing it at the time, he was in the state of existential vacuum described in logotherapy.

And then along came this unpopular—even despised, ridiculed, and contemptuously abhorred—radical little religious sect, which occupied about the same status in Jewish society of that time as does the Communist party in American society today. At first violently opposed to it, and having an official commission to stamp it out, Paul (then Saul of Tarsus) found in the contact with these dedicated people he was liquidating the sense of purpose and meaning that had been missing in his own life. He then "threw in" with them and became a completely new man—in name, in life style, and even in death style.

For his newly found cause, he sacrificed family and friends, material possessions, life comforts, and eventually life itself. But he had found something he had never had before, in spite of all of his material good fortune: a meaning and purpose that made life worth living and—when the time came—death worth dying. He had become a truly committed man.

The second illustration of commitment is an incident involving a member of the Communist Youth Movement in America. This group is, of course, antireligious and atheistic. The use of this example should not be construed as a position favoring the Communist ideology. That you must evaluate for yourself, depending upon whatever personal meanings you hold in the socioeconomic realm. The illustration is, as already noted, offered here only to show that equal degrees of meaning and purpose in life and of commitment to these meanings may be found in people who espouse opposite and contradictory goals. Logotherapy seeks to serve all people equally.

Some years ago, a congressional committee was investigating Communist party activities in America. In the course of the investigations, it called as a witness a member of the Communist Youth Movement in America. At the hearing, this young man made an impassioned speech that was very similar, in reflection of dedication to the cause in which he believed, to the eloquent speech of Paul the Apostle before Agrippa, after which the latter official said, "Almost thou persuadest me to become a Christian."

This young Communist's speech, which was later read into the *Congressional Record* by a member of the committee, ran in part as follows:

> What seems of first importance to you is to me either not desirable or impossible of realization. But there is one thing that I am in dead earnest about, and that is the Communist cause. It is my life, my religion, my business, my hobby, my sweetheart, wife and mistress, my bread and meat. I work at it in the daytime and dream of it at night. Its hold on me grows . . . as time goes on. I'll be in it the rest of my life. It is my altar-ego [sic]. When you think of me it is necessary to think of Communism as well, because I am inseparably bound to it . . . . I have already been in jail because of my ideas, and if necessary I am ready to go before a firing squad. [This] . . . life is no bed of roses. A genuine radical lives in virtual

poverty. He turns back to the Party every penny he makes above what is absolutely necessary to keep him alive . . . . Radicals don't have the money for many movies or concerts or T-bone steaks, decent homes and new cars. We have been described as fanatics. We are. Our lives are dominated by one great overshadowing factor—the struggle for Communism. Well, that's what my life is going to be . . . . We Communists have a philosophy of life no amount of money could buy. We have a cause to fight for, a definite purpose in life . . . . We have a devotion to our cause that no religious order can touch . . . . [Quoted in "Life Line" radio program no. 174-61, June 23, 1961.]

We may disagree with the young man's last statement as we compare his zeal with that of Paul and other religious leaders; but we can certainly see that he has found a meaning and purpose for his own life to which he is fully committed, and that this commitment can match that of religious or other causes.

Prior to the last two generations, and to a considerable extent prior to our own generation, the male in our society got his meaning and purpose in life chiefly from his occupation, while the female got the same from her status as wife, mother, and homemaker. But then the Great Depression and later World War II removed a large segment of American women from the home and put them into occupational competition with men.

America's greatness was built upon the work ethic under which everyone found something meaningful to do, and under which all took pride in doing it, whether in the world of business and industry or in the home. But current socioeconomic conditions have to a large extent destroyed this meaning because it is hard to take pride in a product that is assembly-line produced.

The work ethic has been weakened to the point of near disappearance. As a result, we have relatively few people today who are truly committed to a goal of any kind. All of which points up the widespread need for the message of logotherapy. If we are to regain our greatness as a nation, we must return to the sense of a significant task to do in life as the instrument of meaning, and to awareness of someone for whom to do it as the core of meaning. This implies that the activity has to be productive in terms of fulfilling some human need. To do this is to return to the work ethic that is the key to greatness.

Since we are a nation of individuals (and ours, of all nations, was built upon the foundation of individuality as the prerequisite to meaning), we must each look for our own "bag." But in finding it, we must be aware that it has to yield sufficient personal identity, and to fulfill our personal value needs sufficiently well, to motivate us to make this genuine commitment to it.

We need a commitment such as our forefathers had in relation to the values that gave life meaning to them. Such commitment was the reason why the great majority of them had the courage to face life and to carry on under adversity without copping out through alcohol or other drugs, or through other means of escape from reality. And this is the only thing that can give us the same courage.

You must now have a clear picture of what commitment means. I hope you also have a clear view of some personal goals that generate this commitment in yourself. It may help to see in the next chapter how others have been able to succeed in doing this through logotherapy.

Chapter 11

Evidence
That It
All Works

You will naturally wonder how effective the procedures of logotherapy are with other people. I have been using these procedures with various types of patients, including those with alcoholic problems, for sixteen years, and I have been applying them with special groups of problem drinkers for ten years.

The hospital where I practice clinical psychology has an alcoholic treatment and rehabilitation unit, in which I conduct regular logotherapy groups. I apply my own special techniques of logoanalysis (as described in chapter 9). I have the group members work individually through the book, chapter by chapter, but we discuss the chapter contents in class and exchange ideas. I summarize the main points of each chapter and then ask for discussion from the members. We do the exercises in the back of the book, which parallel the principles presented in the text. The general process is the same as that presented in the present book, except for use of the specific exercises of logoanalysis. Some of these exercises are repeated in the present book, and you could apply the same general principles without the additional exercises, though the exercises make it all simpler, clearer, and easier.

The groups sometimes have only a couple of people, sometimes as many as ten, with an average of five. They meet four times a week in two-hour sessions, for three weeks, and are "closed-end"—that is, all members start and stop together. At the end of the three weeks, a certificate is issued to those who have finished the exercises.

It is not expected that members will magically find new meanings in life in the short span of three weeks. The goal is rather to help each individual to "get on the road" to a new life purpose, to find his basic orientation and direction, and to be aware of what he yet has to do in order to complete the job. The truth is that, as Frankl has pointed out, logotherapy is really complete only in death. We never achieve *all* our goals and should not expect to, lest we experience a big letdown of emptiness at the end. Rather, the aim is to always have viable subgoals in keeping with an overall life purpose.

It would not be surprising if no measurable effects from logotherapy were observed during so short a course, but we do have some. First, in the experimental direction, we have administered the Purpose in Life Test (see chapter 4) before and after both logotherapy and the general Alcoholic Rehabilitation Program (ARP). The logotherapy patients show more improvement at the end of treatment than do patients who are only in the ARP, even though the latter program is six weeks long. Of course, it should be noted that the logotherapy patients are specially selected for probability of success in logotherapy, on the criteria of a good clear mind, reasonably bright intellect, some background of intellectual interests, and some motivation to find something better in life. And this test is designed to measure the kind of changes expected in logotherapy. It all simply means that logotherapy does, at least to some extent, produce more changes in attitudes along the lines expected than are coincidentally produced by the ARP as a whole.

This general ARP is a program with daily morning lectures and movies on various aspects of alcoholism, with afternoon group therapy and adjunctive occupational and physical therapy, and Alcoholics Anonymous contacts. Although it runs for six weeks ordinarily, repeaters may be treated for a shorter period. The program is based on the concept that the alcoholic must abstain completely and permanently from all use of alcohol in order to expect a lasting recovery. The type of ARP is probably not particularly important as far as the effectiveness of logotherapy is concerned, because a patient who is suitable for logotherapy could likely be selected from any program and treated by Frankl's approach with essentially the same results.

Experimental evidence is what impresses scientists, but it is probably less important than clinical evidence of how individual patients respond. Experimental studies are based on statistics that apply to groups that have little meaning as far as you as an individual are concerned. Nobody can be sure that, because others respond well to a given approach, you will too. The only way you can know for sure is to try it. But naturally you would hesitate to invest the necessary time and effort unless you had some reason to think that there was at least a good chance it would work. I feel that the evidence for this is quite strong from both experimental findings and clinical experience.

Clinically the support comes from such statements as the following, gathered independently of my work by the director of the overall program. Among the statements written to him by "graduates" of my segment of the Alcoholism Treatment and Rehabilitation Program were the following:

"I cannot express enough praise for the course in logotherapy."

"As Ph.D. Crumbaugh has stated, 'He who has a Why in life can stand any How.' (Quotation from Nietzsche.) I now have my Why, so I won't worry about my How. . . . It requires positive action as well as positive thinking, which I have now gained, thanks to Ph.D. Crumbaugh and others."

"I hope you get as much out of Dr. Crumbaugh as I did." (Note left in a copy of the logoanalysis book.)

". . . the logotherapy course is most beneficial and helpful in restoring one's self-confidence to carry on in life with hope. . . . "

"I am leaving here with a purpose in my life, for the first time in my life, thanks to Dr. Crumbaugh and logoanalysis."

"One of the highest and most interesting therapy courses was the course in logotherapy, *Everything to Gain,* taught by the learned Dr. James C. Crumbaugh."

"I have been accepted in the Alcoholic and Drug Counselor Training Program at Ft. Lyon. It is through the study of logoanalysis which I participated in last fall with you that I have been able to maintain my sobriety and realize this goal. . . . I feel that you have been a significant influence on my life and I want to thank you for it."

Almost a year later this same ex-patient wrote, "Just a few lines to let you know I am still practicing the principles of logoanalysis . . . . I was to experience a beautiful encounter with a lovely person this past summer . . . . I am Somebody . . . . I wanted to share my happiness with you for you are the one who put me in the right direction . . . . "

Another wrote: "I returned [home] to find all of my old problems, but new ways to cope with them, with logotherapy removing the doubt. By putting it into use, a method that is simple has presented itself."

"I am taking the time . . . to let you know that logotherapy is playing an important role in my life . . . . It is the only thing [to which] I attribute the continuing success of my being sober." (A letter to me about six weeks after discharge.)

A Florida guidance clinic project director writes: "David _____ asks me to advise you of his progress. . . . Rarely have I seen such a dramatic change in a client's attitudes, perceptions and behavior. . . . Dave gives you and your program considerable credit for this change. We have raised the fruit from the seed you planted." An alcohol counselor of the same clinic, at which this ex-patient has now become involved in the residential treatment program, writes: "Dave has frequently mentioned your program. . . . He seems quite enthusiastic about your logotherapy and has recommended your book. . . . I'm sure your program has a great deal to do with laying the groundwork in alcohol education. . . ."

The nearest thing to a criticism written by anyone who had taken the logotherapy course was, "The logo group needs a ten-minute break at mid-period." (Actually this was always done whenever requested, but some groups preferred to go straight through, so it was left up to the group members. In this case, no request had been made until the completion of the course.)

There may have been many who had criticisms but did not voice them. And certainly a fair share of the plaudits went to the other therapy programs, such as a self-esteem group conducted by one of the chaplains, and therapy groups conducted by a psychologist, a social worker, and registered nurses, to mention only a few of the leading activities offered the patients. The physician-director of the unit seemed to be the staff member most popular with the patients. Many of the logotherapy patients expressed appreciation for and enjoyment of the program at its conclusion but showed that they had grasped few of its concepts and had done little related thinking that would help them in the future. On the average, no more than 20 percent of the patients in the Alcoholism Treatment and Rehabilitation Program were selected for logotherapy in the first place, and of this number, one or sometimes two in ten would drop out after a session or two or would refuse to accept the assignment upon being selected for it. Of those who completed the course, probably no more than 50 percent really took with them any permanent influence that would help them stay dry in the future. There were, however, some who showed a deep influence from logotherapy, although some of these did not manifest the desired external signs of recovery. For example, one ex-patient went back to drinking shortly after discharge, but while in attendance at an outpatient clinic, he told his therapist a great deal about logotherapy and how it had influenced his thinking. He thought it had helped him, even though he was not "cured."

Suppose only one patient in each logotherapy group were genuinely helped toward permanent sobriety. Would the program still be worth what it costs? Of course that depends upon how much you figure a life is worth. And that may depend on whose life it is. If it's that of a person next door, perhaps not much. But if it's your life, it's worth quite a lot.

The important question is, Will *you* get help from logotherapy? As mentioned in the preface, it is not for everybody. Nothing works for everybody. But if you really want help, and if you've got a clear and reasonably bright mind and are willing to use it, you can receive help through following the plan presented in this book. How much help will depend on individual factors within you, not the least of which is how hard you are willing to work at it.

Chapter 12

The Challenge:
Now It's Your Move

You have now read about the causes and treatment of problem drinking, the physiological and medical side of alcoholism, and the psychological side. The last includes the factors of motivation that play a key
role in recovery, the logotherapy of Viktor E. Frankl and his thesis that
finding a purpose in life constitutes the essential factor in motivation,
the steps in the application of logotherapy, my own modification of it
called logoanalysis, and what it means to find a purpose to which you
can really dedicate your full capacities and energies. You have seen
how others have found through logotherapy the strength to go on and
to face life without alcohol or other copouts.

Now it's your turn to make a decision for your own life. If you have
read this far, it is assumed that you have bought at least the general
approach of logotherapy, and that you are sold on the connection
between having a deep sense of purpose in life and staying dry. (And if
your problem is not alcohol but some other psychological means of
escape from or defense against the difficulties of the world of reality,
the basic problem in correcting it is still the same: you have to find a
life meaning strong enough to motivate your giving up unhealthy and
inefficient techniques of escape and defense, a motive strong enough to
get you to do whatever you have to in order to give yourself the best
chance of successfully attaining the meaning.)

Presumably, at this point you have worked through the exercises
given for each basic step in attaining a genuine meaning and purpose in

life; and if so, you should, of course, have now at least tentatively identified a strong meaning that motivates you. But I know from experience that many readers will go all the way through the book before deciding what—if anything—they are going to do about the problems involved.

So if you are in this category, you will need now to go back to the start and work step by step right on through the book—if you really want the help it can afford. But no matter what your situation, you will not find any real relief until you are ready. And this does not mean ready to receive help, but ready to help yourself.

The real nitty-gritty work is something no one can do for you; only you can do it for yourself. Others can guide, encourage, cajole, even browbeat or coerce you (for example, a boss who tells you to get help or else); but when the chips are down, only you hold the key to your future success, because only you can force yourself to accept and make use of the help that another person might offer you.

This is another way of saying that only you can control your own free will. We have already seen evidence of that fact, in spite of the contrary opinions of such conditioning psychologists as B. F. Skinner and the behavior modification therapists. Logotherapy holds that, although *conditions* are determined by heredity and environment, the way you face them is your personal free choice.

Therefore no one can force upon you the motivation to want or receive help or guidance, the motivation to follow logotherapeutic or any other techniques in an effort to find something meaningful in life and thereby to lose the need for escape. No one can brainwash you into finding meaning if you don't want it.

The conditioning people can, if given the right opportunity (in the fashion of George Orwell's *1984*) mold your *behavioral* responses in almost any direction. But they cannot mold your will, your attitudes toward what they make you do, unless they destroy your mind completely. You remain free—as long as you are conscious and rational—to drop all desire to find a meaning and purpose in life on the one hand, or to pursue this goal with deep commitment on the other. So you stand at the crossroads in this respect, and only you can choose the direction in which you will go.

The methods of logotherapy are primarily aimed at motivating you through aiding in the opportunities to perceive new meanings that will challenge you. Once most people see new hope, their motivation will rise to meet the challenge of its fulfillment. But *logotherapy cannot furnish the motivation to be motivated!* That is, it cannot make you want to find a meaning and purpose in life if you have exercised your free will to choose not to have any such meaning and purpose.

A psychiatrist I know happens to believe there is no intrinsic meaning and purpose in human life. Unlike the philosopher Jean-Paul Sartre—who believes the same but charges man to find his own personal meanings and add them to a meaningless world—this psychiatrist resists the whole idea of trying to find meaning in life. He is oriented strictly toward personal pleasure, which, logotherapy teaches, is really a copout: when we don't see any meaning in life, we try to escape this grim reality and keep our minds off it by hedonistic satiation.

This psychiatrist says he is perfectly happy. Some who know him doubt it. If, however, a person says he likes himself and his life as it is, and does not wish any change, we cannot say his approach is wrong for him—not even if he is Hitler! We can say only that this kind of life does not appeal to us; and we can add that he must accept responsibility for his choice, and with it the consequences it brings.

If he likes all of this, he has the freedom to make this choice. Nobody can force him to choose differently, and logotherapy cannot motivate him to find meaning in life if he is motivated not to do so.

Therefore, if you really don't want a life meaning, forget about logotherapy. But most people do, and Frankl believes this is really the strongest human motive. Of course a few people may not have this drive to any great extent, just as they may not have much of a sex drive. In the majority of cases, however, with reference both to sex and to the will to meaning, the desire is potentially there, but it is covered up by frustrations and failures.

Hans Strupp and Suzanne Hadley of Vanderbilt University, writing in *The American Psychologist* (March 1977), say that "in increasing numbers, patients enter psychotherapy not for the cure of traditional 'symptoms' but (at least ostensibly) for the purpose of finding meaning in their lives, for actualizing themselves, or for maximizing their potential." (We have learned earlier that one cannot *directly* succeed in seeking self-actualization or happiness, but that these effects follow from having a meaningful life purpose.)

The chances are that these are the things you want out of life. If so, and if you are willing to work at achieving them, the procedures of this book can help you.

And if you really desire recovery from an alcohol problem, it is essential that you find a vital meaning in life that can motivate you to keep going when the going gets tough. As we have seen, this lack of meaning is a key factor in why so many turn to alcohol in the first place: the alcohol serves as an escape from facing the emptiness, or existential vacuum as Frankl calls it, that results from lack of meaning.

There is something you can do that may help you a great deal in the search for meaning. We have already seen in chapter 7 on encounter that the core of meaning lies in our relationship to other beings. So why not involve them from the first in your own search? The old sayings Two heads are better than one, There is safety in numbers, and Misery loves company have application here.

We have noted that, for people with a drinking problem, organizations like AA serve an especially vital need as a source of contact with others of like interests and having the common goal of licking the drinking habit. From the contacts you make in this group or a similar one, you will be able to select certain individuals who show evidence of sharing this common search for a real meaning and purpose in life.

Round up some of these individuals and start a Logotherapy Encounter Group, or "LEG." If you happen to be in psychotherapy while you pursue personal meaning in life by logotherapy through this book, and if your therapist is amenable to the idea, he can set up such a LEG composed of patients who show logotherapeutic needs. Otherwise start a group yourself.

This is a study group. It is not an "encounter"group of the type that employs small-group dynamics to train members to communicate intimately with each other.

An example of the latter is the type of group sponsored by the well-known Esalen Institute of the Big Sur region of California. Some such groups try to bring people closer together through such activities as nude bathing among groups of mixed sex, and other unconventional forms of behavior. This is supposed to make the participants bosom buddies, intimate friends who really understand each other—even though they may have come into the group off the street, may never have seen each other before, and may never see each other again. To my way of thinking, all of this is pure nonsense, and I believe this kind of so-called therapy is a rapidly passing fad. It misses the point of real encounter, which could take place between persons on different planets if the conditions for true interpersonal interaction and relationship were right.

No, we are not talking about this sort of "encounter" here. We are concerned with encounter as defined in chapter 7, and while often the "weirdo" approaches try to sound as if they were aiming at the same, they seldom make it.

We are herein sponsoring a type of get-together to pursue a common interest, and this experience should in many cases cause at least some members of the group to find a valid encounter in our sense with at least some other members. But the central goal is mutual assistance in exploring all possible life values: the intent here is that each individual member come up with something that provides his own personal meaning and purpose, something that will challenge him to do his best in life—that will motivate him to remain dry and/or to do whatever else he has to in order to achieve this meaning. If he finds such meaning, it will enable him to establish some encounters in his life, but they may or may not be with other members of this same group. All group members should develop a mutual friendship and appreciation for each other; remember, however, that encounter in our sense is much deeper than that.

A good way to proceed is through the following five steps:

1. Select several friends who are interested in finding a meaning and purpose in their lives. Have at least three but no more than ten (preferably five to eight) in the group. If more want to join, the group should split into two groups in order to limit the size of each to the number that can efficiently interact.

2. Have the group meet weekly for an hour or two at the home of each member in turn.

3. The session should be informal, with no officers, dues, or other means whereby a manipulating leader might see an opportunity to gain control to feed his own ego. Here a lesson from the experience of Alcoholics Anonymous is in order. The founders of this movement have pointed to the wisdom of such policies in order to prevent misuse of the group. Let the leader for each session be the one who hosts it for that meeting.

4. Each member should have access to this book and be interested in working through all the exercises. The function of the group is to offer

mutual discussion, suggestions, and encouragement to each individual member in completing his exercises. As a member finishes, sets life goals, and demonstrates commitment to them, he is in a "graduate" position to be of maximum help to the other members.

5. If several groups are formed in the community, a joint meeting every couple of months (which will probably require obtaining club quarters for the occasion) will be mutually beneficial. At these meetings, the program should center on a talk by some member on some aspect of the problems he has experienced in completing one of the steps of logoanalysis, and the solutions he has found. Groups should take turns in furnishing a speaker for these joint sessions.

One question you will have to deal with is whether to have a continuous, "open-end" group (that is, a group that new members may enter from time to time, and from which old members will drop for various reasons) or a "closed-end" group (that is, a group wherein all members start together, work through the book together, and then terminate at the same time, although some may be lost along the way for unavoidable reasons). Each approach has advantages and disadvantages.

The "open-end" group has the advantage of being able to accommodate new members at any time if there is room, but the disadvantage of having to stop and orient each new member to the entire procedure. The new admission has to pick up the currently studied chapter as best he can and then continue beyond the last chapter into the fresh start of the book until he reaches where he entered. This is like coming in at the middle of a movie. It is always possible, of course, to remain through to the end a second time.

The "closed-end" group has the advantages of greater group cohesiveness, of better organization through the logical unfolding in sequence of each step in the search for meaning, and of something like the group esprit de corps that always occurs among members of a "class" or unit that starts and completes some task together. Its disadvantage is, of course, that it cannot accommodate new members, who must wait for the formation of a new group.

I have worked with both types of groups in logotherapy. While the closed-end approach has the greatest over-all effectiveness, in some situations it is not practical.

As you start a new group, the "charter members" will have to decide which way to structure it. If you go the open-end route, you may wind up with a situation in which everyone but one or two new entries "graduates;" and these may not be capable of carrying on alone or of building up the group. On the other hand, choosing the closed-end method will leave nothing continuing, unless during the sessions other prospective members decide to start their own group. The best way of handling the problem in a charter group is to discuss these pros and cons and then take a vote on which way to go.

In either approach the principles of procedure stated in the foregoing five steps will pertain. And in both there is no reason why members should not repeat the entire process if they have worked through the book and still not found a real life meaning which challenges their commitment. In the closed-end case they would have to start with a new group; in the open-end situation, they could merely "stay for the show a second time." Many people really require a second round; the principles of learning are such that all of us get more out of a repeated experience.

Every meeting should offer each member (of either type of group) a chance to discuss his own feelings about the material at hand. Each should be encouraged to offer his personal interpretation of the chapter material and to relate his own experience in applying the principles of the chapter then being studied.

And here is where you can exercise your real creative capacities: after the group has done enough of the exercises to get the feel of them, especially those in chapter 8 on exploring the areas of value to find a meaningful activity for one's own life, get each member to make up a new exercise along the same general lines. Then have all members do these new exercises and report on them at a future meeting. It might require several meetings to cover them all.

I know from experience that group members often devise excellent exercises, and while I have not yet reported these in my books, I hope to do so in future work. I will be most interested in any exercises that you or others may care to send me. If you would like to have them published, send them with a statement releasing to me the right to include them in future material. I will try them out with a group; and if they seem to work, I will include them with full credit to you. You can address me through the publisher, Nelson-Hall Company.

A final word of caution: it is always wise to have more than one goal, although the goals usually should be related or in the same general family of life meanings. The reason is that, if for some reason one goal should prove unattainable, you can then switch to pursuit of the other without loss of purpose in life. Frankl has pointed out that despair is the result of one's having placed all of his eggs of energy in one basket of meaning; if this is shattered, he is lost and left with an emptiness of purpose. But if you have a "spare" to fulfill the same underlying human need, you can change goals and still travel without interruption on down the same road to self-fulfillment in the attainment of a life mission that will mark you as Somebody.

Well, isn't it now about time to get along with the whole program of finding meaning and purpose in your life? Depending upon how far you have come as you read this part of the book, you may have a long or a short way yet to go.

However far this may be, I—and my co-authors, Doctors Wood and Wood, who wrote the first section of the book on the medical and physiological aspects of problem drinking—wish you all of the luck in the world. As we have said earlier, the choice is now yours as to what you will do with your life. We hope you will choose to climb the ladder of success. It is steep, and sometimes a rung is missing here and there; but you can make it if you try. If you do try, you will find in logotherapy the steps that can lead you up.

As you see yourself succeeding, we hope you'll let us know. It is important to us, because your success is our only success in the writing of this book. In the meantime we will say, not goodbye, but—

Pax vobiscum
(Peace be with you).

Notes

Chapter 2

1. J. A. Bishop, "Alcohol and Aviation," *Aeromedical Reviews* 3 (July 1975): 1-28.
2. Ibid.
3. A. M. Freedman, H. I. Kaplan, and B. J. Sadock, *Comprehensive Textbook of Psychiatry,* 2d ed. (Baltimore: The Williams and Wilkins Co., 1975).
4. Robert C. Petersdorf, *Harrison's Principles of Internal Medicine,* 7th ed. (New York: McGraw-Hill, 1974).
5. Frederick C. Redlich and Daniel X. Freedman, *The Theory and Practice of Psychiatry* (New York: Basic Books, 1966).

Chapter 4

1. The professionally trained practitioner may wish to examine this literature. To him the Purpose-in-Life Test is available, with a complete manual of instructions, norms, technical data, and bibliography of technical articles on logotherapy, from the publisher: Psychometric Affiliates, Post Office Box 3167, Munster, IN 46321.
2. Viktor E. Frankl, *The Will to Meaning: Foundations and Applications of Logotherapy,* p. 143 (New York: New American Library in association with World Publishing Co., 1969).
3. Ibid., pp. 152–53.

4. Portions of this report of Frankl's logotherapeutic interviews with this patient are quoted by permission of the editor and publisher from: V. E. Frankl, "Fragments from the Logotherapeutic Treatment of Four Cases," in *Modern Psychotherapeutic Practice,* ed. Arthur Burton (Palo Alto, Calif.: Science and Behavior Books, 1965).

Bibliography

In this brief bibliography of books on logotherapy and its background in existentialism, entries marked by asterisk are suitable for the beginner. Readers without any background in the field should undertake first the entries double starred, then those starred once, and finally those unstarred.

Logotherapy

**Crumbaugh, James C. *Everything to Gain: A Guide to Self-Fulfillment through Logoanalysis.* Chicago: Nelson-Hall, 1973.

**Fabry, Joseph B. *The Pursuit of Meaning.* Boston: Beacon Press, 1968; paperback edition, *A Guide to the Theory and Application of Viktor E. Frankl's Logotherapy,* 1969.

*Frankl, Viktor E. *The Doctor and the Soul: An Introduction to Logotherapy.* Translated by Richard and Clara Winston. New York: Alfred A. Knopf, 1955. 2d ed., 1965.

**Frankl, Viktor E. *From Death-Camp to Existentialism.* Translated by Else Lasch. Boston: Beacon Press, 1959. Revised and reissued as *Man's Search for Meaning: An Introduction to Logotherapy,* 1962;

*Frankl, Viktor E. *Psychotherapy and Existentialism.* New York: Washington Square Press, 1967.

*Frankl, Viktor E. *The Will to Meaning: Foundations and Applications of Logotherapy.* New York: New American Library, 1968.

*Frankl, Viktor E. *The Unconscious God.* New York: Simon & Schuster, 1975.

*Frankl, Viktor E. *The Unheard Cry for Meaning: Psychotherapy and Humanism.* New York: Simon and Schuster, 1978.

Leslie, Robert C. *Jesus and Logotherapy.* Nashville: Abingdon Press, 1965.

*Tweedie, Donald F., Jr. *Logotherapy and the Christian Faith.* Grand Rapids: Baker Book House, 1961; paperback edition, 1965.

*Tweedie, Donald F., Jr. *The Christian and the Couch: An Introduction to Christian Logotherapy.* Grand Rapids: Baker Book House, 1963.

Ungersma, A. J. *The Search for Meaning.* Philadelphia: Westminister Press, 1961; paperback edition, 1968.

Existentialism

Allen, E. L. *Existentialism from Within.* New York: Macmillan, 1953.

Barrett, William, *Irrational Man: A Study in Existential Philosophy.* Garden City, N.Y.: Doubleday, 1958.

*Barrett, William. *What Is Existentialism?* New York: Grove Press, 1964.

Binswanger, Ludwig. *Being-in-the World.* Translated by Jacob Needleman. New York: Basic Books, 1963.

*Blackham, H. J. *Six Existentialist Thinkers.* New York: Harper & Bros., 1952.

*Blackham, H. J. *Reality, Man and Existence: Essential Works of Existentialism.* New York: Bantam Books, 1965.

Buber, Martin. *Two Types of Faith.* Translated by Norman P. Goldhawk. New York: Harper & Bros., 1961. (First published in English by Macmillan in 1951.)

*Collins, James. *The Existentialists.* Chicago: Regnery, 1952. (Includes selected bibliography on existentialism.)

*Earle, William, Edie, James M., and Wild, John. *Christianity and Existentialism.* Evanston: Northwestern University Press, 1963.

*Grene, Marjorie. *Dreadful Freedom: A Critique of Existentialism.* Chicago: University of Chicago Press, 1948.

*Grene, Marjorie. *Introduction to Existentialism*. Chicago: University of Chicago Press, 1948.

Harper, Ralph. *Existentialism: A Theory of Man*. Cambridge, Mass.: Harvard University Press, 1948.

Heidegger, Martin. *Sein und Zeit*. Halle: Max Niemeyer, 1931.

*Heidegger, Martin. *Essays in Metaphysics*. Translated by Kurt F. Leidecker. New York: Philosophical Library, 1960.

*Heidegger, Martin. *An Introduction to Metaphysics*. Translated by Ralph Manheim. Garden City, N.Y.: Doubleday, 1961. (First published in German in 1953.)

*Heinemann, F. H. *Existentialism and the Modern Predicament*. New York: Harper & Bros., 1953.

Jaspers, Karl. *Man in the Modern Age*. Translated by Eden and Cedar Paul. Garden City, N.Y.: Doubleday, 1951. (First published in German in 1931.)

*Kaufmann, Walter. *Existentialism from Dostoevsky to Sartre*. New York: Meridian Books, 1956.

Kaufmann, Walter. *From Shakespeare to Existentialism*. Garden City, N.Y.: Doubleday, 1959.

Kierkegaard, Søren. *Fear and Trembling* and *The Sickness unto Death*. Translated by Walter Lowrie. Princeton, N.J.: Princeton University Press, 1941. (*Fear and Trembling* originally published in Danish in 1843. *Sickness unto Death* originally published in Danish in 1849.)

Kierkegaard, Søren. *Either/Or*. Vols. 1 and 2. Translated by David F. and Lillian M. Swenson. Garden City, N.Y.: Doubleday, 1951. (First published in English by Princeton University Press in 1943. Originally published in Danish in 1843.)

**May, Rollo, ed. *Existential Psychology*. New York: Random House, 1961. (Includes a comprehensive bibliography on existentialism by Joseph Lyons.)

*May, Rollo; Angel, Ernest; and Ellenberger, Henri F. (Editors). *Existence: A New Dimension in Psychiatry and Psychology*. New York: Basic Books, 1958.

*Michalson, Carl, ed. *Christianity and the Existentialists*. New York: Scribners, 1956.

**Olson, Robert G. *An Introduction to Existentialism*. New York: Dover Publications, 1962.

*Roberts, David. *Existentialism and Religious Belief.* Edited by Roger Haxelton. New York: Oxford University Press, 1957.

Sartre, Jean-Paul. *Existential Psychoanalysis.* Translated by Hazel Barnes. New York: Philosophical Library, 1953.

Sartre, Jean-Paul. *L'Etre et le Neant.* Paris: Librairie Gallimard, 1943. Translated by Hazel Barnes and issued as *Being and Nothingness.* New York: Philosophical Library, 1956.

**Shinn, Roger L. *The Existentialist Posture.* New York: Association Press, 1959.

Thalheimer, Alvin. *Existential Metaphysics.* New York: Philosophical Library, 1960.

*Wahl, Jean. *A Short History of Existentialism.* Translated by Forrest Williams and Stanley Maron. New York: Philosophical Library, 1949.

*Wild, John. *The Challenge of Existentialism.* Bloomington: Indiana University Press, 1959.

**Winn, Ralph B. *A Dictionary of Existentialism.* New York: Philosophical Library, 1960.

Index